Angelika Lang

Exotic Birds

from A to Z

➤ Favorite bird species from around the world
➤ Feeding tips for better health

BARRON'S

Contents

Families

Portraits of Exotic Birds

Around the Bird Home

Appendix

Families

There are huge flocks of birds that
live in cages and aviaries, and
they captivate us with their
colors, their shapes, and their
lighthearted songs. The following
chapter describes the families to
which the birds belong and what
distinguishes them.

Gallinaceous Birds
Phasianidae

The approximately 170 species of gallinaceous birds are distributed nearly all around the world. They usually inhabit open landscapes and avoid deep woods. This order includes starling-size birds such as the Chinese Painted Quail (*Coturnix chinensis*) and very large species such as the Peacock (*Pavo christatus*). They all have a stocky body, a small head with a short, powerful beak, and strong, featherless legs. They are mostly ground dwellers, and that's where they look for most of their food, such as seeds, and insects for the young birds. The food is ground up in the birds' gizzard with the help of small stones. The birds nest on the ground, and the hen takes charge of the incubation duties. The chicks leave the nest at an early age.

Doves
Columbidae

Doves are found worldwide in around 300 variations. They range from the size of sparrows to nearly the size of geese. Many types of doves form flocks when they are not nesting. Most types look for their food, principally seeds, on the ground. The one to two white eggs are often laid in a simple nest made of twigs. The young are at first fed with a cheeselike secretion from the crop, which is referred to as crop milk. A favorite aviary bird is the Diamond Dove (*Geopelia cuneata*).

Parrots
Psittaciformes

The order of parrots (*Psittaciformes*) includes around 350 types of small to fairly large tree-dwelling birds that live primarily in the tropics. They are generally divided into two

The California Quail, an American ground dweller

Crested Parrots
Cockatoos, which also include cockatiels, are medium to large parrots with a powerful beak and a medium to long tail. Their most important visible characteristic is the erectable crest, which distinguishes them among all Psittacidae. Cockatoos raise their crests instantly when they feel disturbed or become agitated. Seven of the eighteen species are threatened.

families: the true parrots (*Psittacidae*) and Cockatoos (*Cacatuidae*; → Tip above). All parrots have a very powerful, hook-shaped beak with a waxy skin. The upper beak is movable and connected to the skull. The beak is used as an additional tool in climbing. The short legs bear four toes: two face forward and two face toward the rear. This enables the birds to climb very well. Parrots live in trees and brushy areas and eat seeds, buds, blossoms, fruits, and nectar. Many types are very colorful, but there are also plain and primarily green-colored parrots. The "hookbills" generally mate for life. Many types are very social and travel around in

frequently noisy flocks outside the breeding season. They nest in cavities they make themselves, or in preexisting ones. The only ones that make communal, freestanding nests of twigs are the Quaker Parakeets (*Myiopsitta monachus*) in South America. Parrots are known for living to old age in captivity: African Grey Parrots (*Psittacus erithacus*) have reportedly lived to the age of fifty, and several cockatoos have even lived to be over a hundred.

> **The happy parakeets are the most beloved of parrots.**

Nowadays the Australian Parakeet (*Melopsittacus undulatus*) has become the most commonly kept type of parrot. It is bred in countless color variations and is often a real star in competitions at bird shows. Even the larger cockatiel (*Nymphicus hollandicus*), which likewise is native to Australia, enjoys great popularity as a cage bird. The African Agapornis and

The pleasant Peach-faced Lovebirds are robust and easy to keep.

the Amazons from South America are also frequently kept as house pets. The aviaries of bird owners also include some large parrots such as the Greater Sulfur Crested Cockatoo (*Cacatua galerita*) and the Aras, such as the Blue and Gold Macaw (*Ara ararauna*), which is native to South America. One group of tropical parrots, the Lorikeets, are particularly favored by bird owners, for many of the fifty-four varieties bear such beautifully colored feathers that it seems as if they have fallen into a bucket of paint. Even within a single species there are differences in color combinations, which can be seen in the twenty-two subspecies of the Green-naped Rainbow Lorikeets (*Trichoglossus haematodus*): the only thing they have in common is the greenish coloration on top. A subspecies from eastern Australia is also called the Swainson's Blue Mountain Lorikeet (*Th. moluccanus*); it is particularly attractive because of the bright blue color on the belly and its breast framed in red and orange-yellow. In some

EXTRA TIP

A Gift for Mimicking and Language

One reason for the great popularity of parrots is their tremendous ability to modulate their voices. Although parrot screeches often sound harsh and scratchy or even unpleasant, the innate ability to imitate sounds and noises is astonishingly well developed in certain species. The African Greys (*Psittacus erithacus*) and some Amazon types are capable of imitating the human voice very effectively.

circles this subspecies is sold as the "Lorikeet from the Blue Mountains." The Lorikeet's most important feature is the brushlike tip of the tongue, which enables it to gather its main food: nectar and pollens.

Hummingbirds
Trochilidae

This bird family contains more than 330 species. Although they are found in the United States, they cannot legally be kept here as pets. However, there is scarcely another bird family that displays such a fantastic array of colors. This family also includes the smallest bird in the world, the Bee Hummingbird (*Calypte helenae*), which weighs just 2 grams. Hummingbirds get their food, which consists

principally of flower nectar, by buzzing in one spot in front of flowers (→ Tip, p. 11).

Pittas
Pittidae

The short-tailed, thrushlike pittas are part of the order of sparrows. They are colorful and conspicuous, and yet they rarely attract attention on the forest floor, where they live. Pittas eat insects, snails, and occasionally small vertebrates. Of the approximately thirty

The White-necked Jacobin is beautifully colored and fairly easy to keep.

> **Red-whiskered Bulbuls enchant with their warbling song.**

species, only the African Pitta lives in Africa. The other species are distributed from South Asia to Australia. Pittas rear their young in rounded nests made of leaves and roots.

Bulbuls
Pycnonotidae

The predominantly plain-colored bulbuls resemble thrushes, a family of songbirds. There are about 125 types that inhabit the tropics and subtropics of

EXTRA TIP

Hummingbirds drink through a "straw."
Although they cannot be kept as pets, many hobbyists enjoy observing them at outdoor feeders. Hummingbirds eat primarily nectar and pollen. To get their food, the front third of their tongue is forked, and each half is rolled up. In addition, the end of the tongue is frayed, and the strands are tiny tubes. When the hummingbird plunges its tongue into the nectar, the fluid rises in the tubes. Then the bird pulls its tongue back into its beak. When the tongue is extended again, the nectar is squeezed out through the small beak.

A favorite guest: a Golden-fronted Leafbird from Southeast Asia.

have shiny black and blue feathers and a red iris. The females have somewhat dull greenish feathers. Except for the Golden-fronted Leafbird (*Chloropsis aurifrons*), which inhabits the deciduous monsoon forests, all species occur in the evergreen rain forest. They usually stay in the treetops. Although Leafbirds eat insects and fruits, bluebirds eat fruits and berries almost exclusively, especially ripe

Asia and Africa. Typical features include the elongated, hairlike feathers on the neck, the short, slightly bent beak, and the powerful legs that allow the birds to climb nimbly in the underbrush. That's where they build their bowl-shaped nests. Their food consists of fruits and insects. Many types of these sociable, often noisy birds wear a crest and have a melodious song.

Bluebirds
Irenidae

Bluebirds are small to medium songbirds with usually beautiful coloration. Their homeland is in Southeast Asia. Whereas the Leafbirds (genus *Chloropsis*) are green and yellow, the true bluebirds (genus *Irena*)

EXTRA TIP

The Effects of Fruit Consumption
Many tropical and subtropical bird species feed primarily on fruits and nectar. As a result their droppings are relatively fluid. To prevent fungus and bacterial infections, the houses of fruit eaters must be cleaned every two to three days, and the floor covering must be changed regularly.

figs. A favorite bird for the aviary is the Asian Fairy Bluebird (*Irena puella*).

Thrushes
Turdidae

The thrushes, which are spread all around the world, include small to medium songbirds with a slender beak and long legs; their main food is insects and other small creatures. They construct bowl-shaped nests, and their young are speckled. True thrushes are

> **Small, but wow: European Robins vehemently defend their territory.**

tree birds, but they seek their food primarily on the ground. The small types such as the European Robin and the Siberian Blue Robin generally live on or near the ground. The White-rumped Shama (*Copsychus malabaricus*) is a favorite cage bird from this large family.

Babblers
Timaliidae

This large family of birds contains around 280 different types; most of them originated in the Old World (that is, Eurasia and Africa), and their greatest concentration is in Southeast Asia. Babblers generally have a powerful beak, short, rounded wings, and strong legs. They run on the ground or climb in low underbrush. As they do so, they call frequently. Many of them live in social bands, which help each other out even with nesting. Their preferred food sources are mainly insects and fruits. Some species of babblers stand out from the unremarkable gray or brown babblers. One of them is the sparrow-sized, beautifully colored Blue-winged Minla (*Leiothrix lutea*), a highly esteemed cage bird. Its loud, conspicuous warbling song is also responsible for its being called the Chinese Nightingale. There is no relationship to the nightingale, however.

Flycatchers
Muscicapidae

The family of flycatchers contains around 400 species of small songbirds that occur only in the Old World, and not in America. An important feature is the way in which the flycatchers get their food. Flycatchers generally perch on an elevated blind and wait for passing insects, which they catch in the air. Their beak is surrounded by short, stiff bristles, and the tip of the beak has a small hook. Bird lovers are especially fond of flycatchers of the genus *Niltava*.

The male and female Blue-winged Minla are hardly distinguishable from each other.

Vitally Important Vitamins and Minerals
All birds must ingest these substances with their food.
Vitamins perform important functions in metabolism; minerals
are used to develop the bone structure, among other things. A
deficiency may lead to many diseases. Vitamins are present in
fruits and vegetables. Vitamin and mineral supplements
provide the birds with what they need in times of heightened
stress.

White-eyes
Zosteropidae

The nearly ninety species of
white-eyes are small
songbirds that live in the
trees in the tropics; they are
similar to Old World
warblers. Not all species
have the ring around the
eyes that gives them their
name. Many white-eyes play
a very important ecological
role as pollinators of various
flowering plants. One
beloved cage bird is the
Oriental White-eye
(*Zosterops palpebrosus*).

Buntings
Emberizidae

About 600 sparrows inhabit
the Old and New Worlds.
They live primarily in open

landscapes and in brushy terrain. Their tough cone-shaped beak can open up hard seeds. In addition, they consume insects, which they also feed to their young. Buntings locate their nests on the ground or low in bushes. The young are quick to leave the nest, even before they are able to fly, and they hide in the vegetation. Males and females of the same species have different coloration. Male buntings often have contrasting, colorful feathers, but the females appear rather inconspicuous. Buntings include the blue finches (*Passerina*), tanagers (*Thraupinae*), and cardinals (*Cardinalinae*), which may not legally be kept as pets in the United States. Bird fanciers esteem them for their beautiful colors.

The male Yellow Hammer is a lively, persistent singer.

EXTRA TIP

Safe Transport
Small birds such as Budgerigars can be transported in a sturdy paper bag or small ventilated cardboard boxes. The container keeps them from flapping around and injuring themselves. Air slits let the bird get adequate oxygen. You can transport larger birds in a cage or travel carrier designed for birds. Take the quickest way home.

Bananaquit
Coerebidae
Many analysts place these songbirds, which cannot legally be kept as pets in the United States, along with tanagers, wood warblers, and even finches. The family consists of just one species, the Bananaquit (*Coereba flaveola*), which inhabits forested areas in Central and South America and the Antilles. In addition to insects, the birds eat mostly flower nectar, which they suck up with their forked tongues that are fringed at the tip.

Finches
Fringillidae

> **Chaffinches are kept as pets because of their beautiful song.**

This family consists of about 125 species. It includes small to medium songbirds with conical, often hefty beaks equipped with sharp cutting edges. The birds use them in part to open hard seeds, which make up the majority of their food. One typical finch trait is the notched, generally small tail. Finches frequent a variety of habitats, from the interior of large forested areas to steppes and deserts. They often build their bowl-shaped nests in trees and

---

EXTRA TIP

The Food Determines the Shape of the Beak

A glance at the more or less cone-shaped beak of fowl, finches, Estrildid finches, and buntings provides an indication of what they eat: seeds. Every bird group uses a different technique. Finches have sharp cutting edges on their lower beak that make it easy to cut into hard seeds. Buntings and Estrildid finches squash seeds by squeezing them against the roof of their mouths. Fowl swallow the seeds whole, and their stomach does the work of grinding them up.

> **The Siskin likes an aviary with lots of evergreens.**

> **The Common Bullfinch is characterized by a black cap.**

bushes. Outside the breeding season the birds travel about in flocks. The most familiar finch is the canary, which has been bred in many colors and varieties for hundreds of years. Its talent for singing is common to many other species in its family. Over many generations it has become particularly refined into the tireless warblers known as Roller Canaries.

Estrildidae
Estrildidae (Waxbills and allies)

The approximately 135 varieties of Estrildidae (Waxbills and allies) are less closely related to the finches than to the weavers. They are distinguished from the

latter particularly by the often close resemblance between males and females. They also lack the sparrowlike stripes and flecking. Estrildid finches are usually brightly colored and offer attractive patterns. They are hardy, undemanding wards that can be bred even by owners with little experience. The birds build covered nests, and many Estrildid finches equip the construction with

EXTRA TIP

Throat Pattern
Young Estrildid finches have a conspicuous dot and line pattern on their throats. This occurs with no other bird family, with the exception of the Indigo birds (*Viduinae*). Indigo birds appear among Estrildidae as nest raiders, and they imitate the throat pattern of the Estrildid finches as well as their behavior.

an entry tunnel. The eggs are always pure white. Estrildid finches live in grassy and brushy terrain and among scattered trees. That's where they find their food, which consists mainly of grass seeds. During the mating season many Estrildid finches consume quite a few insects and other arthropods. Their beaks are made for the task. Most of the species are found in Africa, plus a few in south Asia and Australia. Estrildid finches have become

> The wonderful colors of many Estrildidae are a treat for the eyes.

established in several places in Europe; examples include the Common Waxbill (*Estrilda astrild*) and the Tiger Finch (*Amandava amandava*) in southern Spain and Portugal.

In contrast to many finches, the Estrildidae have only modest singing talent. The Zebra Finch (*Poephila guttata*) enjoys great popularity. It is frequently purchased because it is

particularly robust and prolific, and it has very striking plumage.

Weavers
Ploceidae

This family of songbirds, which also includes sparrows, contains around 160 fairly small species that are mostly indigenous to the Old World. Some species, including the House Finches, have become established in America. Most weaver birds live in

> **At breeding time many male weavers enchant with their "neon" colors.**

Africa south of the Sahara. At breeding time the males of many species put on a remarkably colorful plumage, and this accounts for their favor as cage birds. Most weavers, though, are uniformly gray-brown in color, and the female strongly resembles the female house sparrow. Most species weave artistic covered nests in tall grass, reeds, or bushes and trees.

The curious Superb Starling brings life to the aviary.

Starlings
Sturnidae

The approximately 110 species of starlings around the world were originally found only in the Old World; however, several species have become established in America, Australia, and New Zealand. In these places they found good living conditions, and they have reproduced accordingly. They locate their often untidy nests in trees and holes in cliffs. Starlings are powerfully built, and they have a slender, pointed beak and powerful legs. Many species, such as the Superb Starling (*Lamprotornis superbus*), have beautifully colored, glossy plumage. They feed on insects and worms and fruits. The Brahming Starling (*Sturnus pagodarum*) collects nectar and pollen with its brush-shaped tongue.

Legal Requirements

Bird species from all over the world are included on lists of threatened or endangered species. The main reason for the decline

EXTRA TIP

The Common Hill Mynah—the Language Specialist Among the Starlings
The three subspecies Common Hill Mynah (*Gracula religiosa*)—small, medium, and large—inhabit the mountain forests from Sri Lanka and India to Malaysia and Indonesia. The bright, lively, vocal birds are particularly esteemed because many of them are real masters at imitating human speech—often with an astonishing resemblance to the model. The medium mynahs include some particularly gifted talkers. Young birds learn more readily than older ones.

in species is the destruction of habitat and capture for the pet trade. Numerous laws have been enacted to stop the depletion of nature.

The Washington Species Protection Agreement (WSPA)

The WSPA is the basis for all national and international species protection efforts. It was implemented in 1973 to reduce the commerce in threatened, free-living animal species and plants, as well as products made from them. To date, more than 160 nations worldwide have subscribed to the WSPA. The central elements of the WSPA are three appendices in which species are listed according to their endangered status. Appendix I species are directly threatened with extinction, and commerce involving them is subject to strict regulation.

Removal from natural habitat is permitted only for scientific research. Appendix II species are threatened with possible extinction, and commerce involving them is restricted. Appendix III species are subject to special regulations in individual member nations. Every two years the status of the threat to animals and plants is updated. The trade agreement is known under the acronym CITES, which stands for Convention on International Trade in Endangered Species of Wild Fauna and Flora. A CITES certification is required for import and export of all Appendix I and II species; it allows legal dealings involving a particular species.

Leg Bands

You may see a small band, or ring, on your bird's leg. This is a breeder band, and signifies that the bird was domestically bred. Breeder bands are closed circles of metal, plastic, or other material, and fit loosely over

Most parrots are strictly protected, and that includes the Princess of Wales Parakeet.

Look for Birds Bred in Captivity
In the meantime, the continued existence of many bird species is threatened by capture for the pet trade. There are only about 600 Red Siskins (photo above) still living in the wild, but there are plenty of them in cages and aviaries. Many bird species are sold as having been bred in captivity. These are the ones you should look for. Not only do you protect the wild populations, but the birds bred in captivity are also better acclimatized.

the bird's leg. You will see a series of letters and numbers on a breeder band; this is the breeder's code and helps identify your bird. An open (or "broken") band made of rounded metal is an import band. These bands signify that the bird was legally imported and went through the approved period of quarantine. A series of letters followed by a sequence of numbers appear on import bands. The letters signify the state where the quarantine station is, the station's code, and part of the bird's I.D. number. Importation stopped around 1992, so if someone tries to sell you a "baby" bird wearing an import band, you will know that it most certainly is an older bird.

Not every bird will have a band. Some hobbyist breeders don't band their birds, and some owners prefer to remove the band for various reasons. Always check with your avian veterinarian to verify that an unbanded bird is safe to buy, or before removing your own bird's band. The veterinarian will record the band number and breeder information in your bird's file.

Where to Find an Exotic Bird

Healthy, beautiful exotic birds are available from a number of sources. The obvious places include pet stores, bird specialty stores, and breeders. Most of these birds will already be tame

and sweet. You might also check with bird clubs and other bird owners, as well as the advertisements listed in the backs of many bird-related publications. And do not overlook hobbyists who may raise only a few birds a year, or even previously owned older pet birds However, before purchasing a previously owned bird, find out why the owner is selling it. You don't want to buy a bird that has a screaming habit or other problematic issue.

Budgerigars come in a wide variety of colors.

Selecting a Healthy Bird

> **Most of the colorful Aras are seriously endangered.**

Once you've found a bird you might like to buy, there are a number of ways to determine whether or not it is healthy. Look the bird over carefully. Its eyes should be bright and clear, the nostrils should be open and the feathers around them clean and not crusty or stuck together, the feathers underneath the tail should be clean, not matted together or stained, and the bird should not look too thin. All the feathers should

EXTRA TIP

Who can provide information about the protected status of animals?
You can get further information about protected species and other regulations from the following institutions: the U.S. Fish and Wildlife Service at www.fws.gov; the U.S. Fish and Wildlife Endangered Species Program at www.fws.gov/endangered; the U.S. State and Territory Animal Import Regulations at www.aphis.usda.gov/vs/sregs/; the U.S. Department of Agriculture's (USDA) Animal and Plant Health Inspection Service (APHIS) at www.aphis.usda.gov/.

be glossy and well groomed, and the beak and legs well formed. The bird should be vocal, active, and interested in the things going on around it.

Troublesome Signs

Avoid purchasing a bird that is too quiet, thin, has crusted matter on its face or vent, or is in poor feathering not related to a normal molt. Also, pass up birds that are wheezing, having difficulty breathing, have a nasal discharge, or have swelling around the eyes.

Young Birds

Very young birds might be rough looking; this is normal for healthy baby birds before they have undergone the first molt, or ones that are still being hand-fed. Oftentimes baby birds, especially parrot-types, will chew on their clutch mates' feathers as toys, creating a straggly appearance. In addition, baby birds are typically clumsy. They fall over repeatedly and frequently crash into the cage bars and other objects, damaging their feathers. They may look unkempt and unhealthy, but can be perfectly fine. Because some illnesses may not be obvious, it is always wise to have a qualified avian veterinarian look at any bird you are considering.
Note: molting is the natural process of shedding old feathers and replacing them with new ones. Some birds look ragged and rough during the molt, but this does not mean they are ill. They will return to their former beauty once all their new feathers have grown in.

Considerations

Before you invest in an outdoor aviary, there are a number of important factors that you need to consider. Above all is the climate in which you live.

> **The laughing dove is easy to keep and adapts readily to new situations.**

Approval to Construct an Outdoor Aviary

For some birds, particularly the larger species, an outdoor aviary may be a suitable alternative living arrangement. But before you begin construction, you need to get information on construction regulations from the relevant authorities in your city or town. These vary from location to location; check with your local building and zoning department. You should also find out your neighbors' preferences in advance.

Some birds are more sensitive to weather conditions than others. If you're not sure if your birds can withstand the temperatures and humidity fluctuations that invariaby change with the time of day and months of the year, it's best to check with an avian veterinarian. How many birds you intend to keep and whether you plan on keeping them outdoors year round are other important factors that need to be taken in account. And be sure to have safeguards in place to protect your birds against theft and malicious mischief.

Portraits of Exotic Birds

The 200 most beloved exotic birds
arranged by English name, along
with individual portraits and iden-
tifying features, tips on ownership
and care, plus brief information
on the family to which they
belong.

Explanation of the Portraits

(from pages 32 through 229)

English Name: Common English designation

Scientific Name: Compound name. The first name designates the order, the second the species, and if applicable, the third, a subspecies.

Also: Further English and scientific names, in part because of different classification systems.

Description: Information on traits used to distinguish the sexes, occurrences of colors, information about song and mimicking talent. Typical behavior patterns, such as breeding.

Housing: The type of accommodations, necessary size given in terms of length by width by height, in accordance with suggested minimums. The actual dimensions should be larger than the ones suggested. In every case it would be better to select a larger cage or aviary. Length is more important than width, and for species that climb, increased height is preferable to added width. In general the measurements should correspond to the following ratio: 4:2:3 (length, width, height). Unless specified otherwise, the size refers to a pair of birds. For one or two additional birds, the surface area generally must be increased 25 percent—50 percent in the case of parrots. In addition, information on providing plants and appropriate accessories is provided.

Living Conditions: Information on special living conditions and required care, plus conditions for breeding.

Social Behaviors: Information about keeping birds with others of the same and different species.

Diet: A list of the common types of foods for adult birds.

Quick Info

Systematic classification of the particular species into order and family.

Description of the area of distribution.

Info Boxes

The most important information at a glance concerning housing for birds, degree of difficulty of care, voice, and size. The specific symbols and information are as follows:

➤ Housing

Cage
(→ p. 232)
Indoor aviary
(→ p. 235)
Outdoor aviary
(→ p. 237)

➤ Degree of difficulty

1: Appropriate for beginners
1*: Appropriate for children
2: Appropriate for care providers with previous experience
3: Ownership appropriate only for experienced specialists

➤ Voice

🎵	Good singer
))))	Loud voice
♩	Neutral voice

➤ Size

The dimensions refer to size measured from the tip of the beak to the tip of the tail.

Metric Conversions

See page 250 for the metric equivalents of some of the more common Imperial measures appearing in this book. Additional conversions can be found on the Internet.

African Grey

Psittacus erithacus

Housing: 🏠 🏢
Degree of difficulty: 2
Voice: 🔊
Size: 14–15½ in.

Description: Male and female look the same. High whistle, squawk, piercing alarm call; good imitators. Cavity nester.

Housing: All-steel indoor or outdoor aviary (6×3×3 ft., wire thickness ¾₄ in.) with shelter (3×3 ft., no cooler than 50°F / 10°C). Floor concrete. Natural wood perches and climbing branches; provide opportunities for activities (→ p. 242). Keep food, water, and bathing containers elevated.

Living Conditions: Likes to bathe. Humidity over 60%. Mating pair should be able to select each other from among flock. Nesting cavities in nesting box, natural tree trunk, or wooden barrel (12–14×12–14×24–32 in., entry hole 4–5 in.); put in decayed wood. Two to four eggs, incubation 28–30 days.

Social Behaviors: Single bird with family bond, or may be kept with birds from other species.

Diet: Seed mixture for large parrots, manufactured diets (→ p. 246), sprouted food, green food, vegetables and fruits, dried fruits; fresh twigs for gnawing.

QUICK INFO **Order:** *Parrots* **Family:** *Parrots* (→ p. 6)
Distribution: *Mali, Sierra Leone to Ivory Coast, east to Kenya and Tanzania, south to Zaire.*

African Ring-necked Parakeet

Psittacula krameri

Housing: 🏠 🏢
Degree of difficulty: 1
Voice: 🔊
Size: 14½–17 in.

Description: Female colored like male, but without throat and neck band. Several colors possible. Loud; good imitator. Cavity nester.

Housing: Indoor aviary or outdoor aviary (9×3×6 ft., wire thickness ⁵⁄₆₄ in.) with shelter (6×3 ft., no cooler than 50°F / 10°C). Floor gravel; or concrete with good drainage. Perches and climbing branches; provide opportunities to keep occupied (→ p. 242). Keep food, water, and bathing containers elevated.

Living Conditions: Toes sensitive to cold. Nesting cavity in nesting box or natural tree trunk (10×10×16–20 in., entry hole 3¼ in.), put in some decayed wood or wood shavings. Three to six eggs, incubation 23 days. Reliable nesters.

Social Behaviors: May be kept with several mating pairs and with other birds.

Diet: Several types of millet, canary grass seed, unhusked oats and wheat, seeds containing only a little oil, fruit, sprouted food, egg food, twigs for gnawing; offer manufactured diet.

QUICK INFO **Order:** *Parrots* **Family:** *Parrots* (→ p. 6)
Distribution: *Tropical Africa north of the equator, Sri Lanka, Indian subcontinent to southeastern China.*

African Silverbill

Lonchura cantans

Also: *Euodice cantans*

Description: Male and female look the same. Various colors possible. Soft, whispering, purring song. Lively. Becomes friendly. Open nester.

Housing: Cage/indoor aviary (32×16×16 in.) or outdoor aviary (6×3×6 ft.) with shelter (3×3 ft. at least 59°F / 15°C). Lots of shrubbery and clear ground. Sand floor with good drainage. Provide containers for food, drinking water, and bathing near ground level.

Living Conditions: Twelve- to fourteen-hour days with aid of light. Likes to bathe. Freestanding nest in vegetation; nesting aids: half-open or closed nesting box, nesting basket; nesting material: coconut fibers, hay, grasses, hair, plant wool, feathers. Four to six eggs, incubation approximately 12 days.

Social Behaviors: Peaceable. Possible to keep several pairs, including with other types of finches.

Diet: Large- and small-grained varieties of millet, canary grass seeds, sprouted food, green food; grit in limited amounts.

Housing:

Degree of difficulty: 1

Voice: ♫

Size: 4½ in.

QUICK INFO **Order:** *Sparrows* **Family:** *Estrildidae (Waxbills and allies) (→ pg. 18)* **Distribution:** *Senegal and Mauritania to Ethiopia, in the east from Somalia to Tanzania, southwestern Arabia.*

34

African Yellow White-eye

Zosterops senegalensis

Housing: 🏠 🏠
Degree of difficulty: 2
Voice: 🎵
Size: 4–4½ in.

Description: Male and female look alike. Warbling, twittering song. Open nester.

Housing: Indoor aviary (60×32×48 in.) or indoor aviary with shelter (3×3 ft., no cooler than 68°F / 20°C). Thick vegetation or potted plants. Floor covering birdcage litter. Keep food, water, and bathing containers elevated.

Living Conditions: Clean floor and furnishings every day or two because of runny droppings. Likes to bathe in bowl and damp leaves. Provide twelve-hour day all year. Mating pair should be able to select each other in flock. Freestanding nest in vegetation; nesting aids: nesting basket or half-open nesting box; nest materials: stems, coconut fibers, plant wool, animal hair. Two to four eggs, incubation 11–13 days.

Social Behaviors: Incompatible with other African Yellow White-eyes and other White-eyes. May be kept with birds of other species.

Diet: Nectar solution for White-eyes, fruits and berries, fine soft foods, small live food.

QUICK INFO **Order:** *Sparrows* **Family:** *White-eyes*
(→ p. 15) **Distribution:** *Tropical regions south of the Sahara.*

Alexandrine Parakeet

Psittacula eupatria

Also: Princess of Wales parakeet, Princess Parrot

Housing: 🏠 🏫
Degree of difficulty: 1
Voice: 🔊
Size: 20–25 in.

Description: Female less brightly colored than male, without throat and neck band. Several colors possible. Loud squawk; good imitators. Cavity nester.

Housing: All-metal indoor or outdoor aviary (9×3×6 ft., wire thickness ⁵⁄₆₄ in.) with shelter (6×3 ft., no cooler than 50°F / 10°C). Floor gravel or concrete; good drainage. Branches for climbing and perching; provide ways to keep birds occupied (→ p. 241). Keep food, water, and bathing containers elevated.

Living Conditions: Nesting cavities in hardwood nesting boxes (12×12×24 in., entry hole 4–5 in.); add decayed wood or shavings. Two to four eggs, incubation 28 days. Reliable nesters.

Social Behaviors: Aggressive toward other Alexandrine Parakeets and related species, even in adjacent aviaries. May be kept with Estrildidae, doves, or chickens.

Diet: Seed mixture for large parakeets, manufactured diets (→ p. 246), sprouted, ripe or half-ripe, nuts, green food and carrots, fruits and berries, egg food; branches for gnawing.

QUICK INFO Order: *Parrots* Family: *Parrots* (→ p. 6)
Distribution: *Sri Lanka, eastern Afghanistan and western Pakistan to India and Vietnam, Andaman Islands.*

Australian Ringneck

Barnardius barnardi

Description: Female the same color as the male, but not as bright. Good flier. Cavity nester.

Housing: All-metal indoor or outdoor aviary protected from draft and rain (6×3×3 ft., wire thickness ⁵⁄₆₄ in.) with frost-free shelter (3×3 ft.). Sand floor beneath natural wood branches for climbing and perching. Open dirt or concrete floor. Provide plenty of flying room. Place heavy food, drinking water, and bathing containers close to floor level.

Living Conditions: A robust bird species. Likes to bathe. Mating pair should be able to select each other in flock. Nesting cavities in natural tree trunks or nesting boxes (14×14×24–40 in., entry hole 3½ in.); provide dirt and peat moss. Four to five eggs, incubation 20–21 days.

Social Behaviors: Keep breeding pair by themselves. Keep no other birds of the same or related species in neighboring aviaries because of their argumentative nature.

Diet: Seed mixture for large parakeets, manufactured diets (→ p. 246), plenty of sprouts and green food, fruit and berries; fresh twigs for gnawing.

Housing: 🏠 🏠
Degree of difficulty: 2
Voice: ♩
Size: 13 in.

QUICK INFO Order: *Parrots* **Family:** *Parrots* (→ p. 6)
Distribution: *Eastern Australia, not on coast.*

Bare-eyed Cockatoo

Cacatua sanguinea

Description: Male and female look the same. Loud voice, good imitator. Likes to dig and climb. Cavity nester.

Housing: All-metal indoor or outdoor aviary (6×3×3 ft., mesh size 1½ in. square, wire thickness ⅛–³⁄₁₆ in.) with shelter (3×3 ft., no cooler than 59°F / 15°C). Concrete floor with 6 in. sand-dirt mixture. Branches for perching and climbing; opportunities to keep occupied (→ p. 242). Food, water, and bathing containers on wall.

Living Conditions: Spray or sprinkle regularly. Change floor covering yearly. Check regularly for worms. Nesting cavity in natural tree trunk, nesting box, or wooden barrel (14 gallons, inside diameter 14 in., depth 24–32 in., entry hole 4–5 in.). Three to four eggs, incubation 21–24 days.

Social Behaviors: Keep mating pair by themselves during breeding season. Keep only individual bird with parrots of equal size.

Diet: Seed mixture for cockatoos, manufactured diets (→ p. 246), sprouted food, fruits, vegetables, green food; softwood branches for gnawing.

Housing: 🏠 🏢
Degree of Difficulty: 2
Voice: 🔊
Size: 15 in.

QUICK INFO **Order:** *Parrots* **Family:** *Cockatoos* (→ p. 7) **Distribution:** *All of Australia as far as the eastern and southern coasts, New Guinea.*

Blackbird

Turdus merula

Also: *Merula merula*

Description: Male black, female brownish. Melodious, warbling song. Open nester.

Housing:	
Degree of Difficulty: 1	
Voice:	♫
Size: 10–11 in.	

Housing: Cage (32×16×16 in.) or outdoor aviary with frost-free shelter (3×3 ft.). Half with clear floor, half covered with small trees or bushes. Floor lined with absorbent paper and sand in cage. Place drinking and bathing containers on floor.

Living Conditions: Easy to care for, undemanding. Likes to bathe. Change floor covering every one to two days. Freestanding nest in vegetation or among twigs; nesting aid: nesting basket, small flat box; nest materials: twigs, plant fibers, grasses, roots, loamy earth, moss. Four to six eggs, incubation 12–14 days.

Social Behaviors: Occasionally quarrelsome with other blackbirds during breeding time. May be kept in an aviary with other seed eaters. May be kept alone in a cage.

Diet: Coarse soft food for thrushes, green food and vegetables, berries, fruit, grit or cuttlebone.

QUICK INFO **Order:** *Sparrows* **Family:** *Thrushes* (→ p. 13) **Distribution:** *Nearly all of Europe as far as the Urals, North Africa, Near East to China.*

Black-capped Conure

Pyrrhura rupicola

Description: Males and females look the same. Strong fliers. Quiet voice. Hard chewers.

Housing: Cage or indoor aviary (18×18×24 in.); outdoor aviary (9×3×6 ft.). Branches for chewing and perching. Provide food, water, and bathing containers off the ground; nest box for sleeping.

Living Conditions: Avid bathers. Cavity nesters. Breeds readily. Attach next box high in enclosure. Wooden box (10×10×10 in.), pine shavings. Four to eight eggs, incubation 23–25 days.

Social Behaviors: Territorial of cage. Can be aggressive to other birds, regardless of species or size.

Diet: Seed mixture for large parakeets, manufactured diets, fresh fruits and vegetables, nuts, sprouts. Supply cuttlefish, mineral, and vitamin supplements.

Housing:
Degree of difficulty: 2
Voice:
Size: 10 in.

QUICK INFO Order: *Parrots* Family: (→ p. 6) *Parrots*
Distribution: *Bolivia, Brazil, Peru.*

Black-capped Lory

Lorius l. lory

Housing: ▦ 🏠 🏘
Degree of Difficulty: 2
Voice: 🔊
Size: 12¼ in.

Description: Males and females look the same. Swift fliers; noisy; sometimes utters whistling vocalizations; active. Can be hard chewers.

Housing: Cage or indoor aviary (24×24×36 in.); outdoor aviary (12×3 ×6 ft., at least 64°F / 18°C). Provide food and water containers off the floor; branches for chewing; swings for playing and perching; nest box for sleeping.

Living Conditions: Provide wooden nest box (16×8×12 in.). One to two eggs; incubation 25 days.

Social Behaviors: Compatible with other birds, playful, energetic; can be aggressive to other birds when breeding.

Diet: Commercially prepared lory diets, fresh fruits and vegetables, flowers, some sprouted seeds; offer calcium supplements.

QUICK INFO **Order:** *Psittaciformes* **Family:** *Loriidae*
Distribution: *New Guinea.*

Black-cheeked Lovebird

Agapornis nigrigenis

Housing:			
Degree of Difficulty: 1			
Voice:			
Size: 5½ in.			

Description: Male and female look the same. Twittering voice. Cavity nester.

Housing: Cage or indoor aviary (36× 18×18 in., wire thickness ¾₄ in.) with shelter (3×3 ft., no cooler than 41°F / 5°C). Floor sand. Branches for perching and climbing; opportunities to keep occupied (→ p. 242). Place food, water, and bathing containers near ground level.

Living Conditions: When kept in cage, daily free flight. Likes to bathe. Mating pair should be able to select each other in flock. Nesting hole in natural tree trunk (25×6×8 in., entry hole 2 in.); put in damp peat moss; nest materials: pieces of bark, twigs, and leaves. Five to six eggs, incubation 21–22 days.

Social Behaviors: Flock may be kept in large aviary; keep mating pair by themselves in a cage.

Diet: Seed mixture for parakeets; offer manufactured diets; (→ p. 246), foxtail millet, sprouted food, fruits, vegetables, green food; cuttlebone; twigs for gnawing.

QUICK INFO **Order:** *Parrots* **Family:** *Parrots* (→ p. 6)
Distribution: *Namibia, Zambia, Zimbabwe, and Botswana.*

Black-chinned Yuhina

Yuhina nigrimenta

Housing:
Degree of Difficulty: 2
Voice: 🎵
Size: 4 in.

Description: Male and female look the same. Three-syllable, warbling song with purring trill at the end. Becomes friendly. Curious. Cavity nester.

Housing: Indoor or outdoor aviary (6×3×6 ft.) with shelter (3 x 3 ft., no cooler than 68°F / 20°C). Lush planting. Floor lined with birdcage litter. Keep food, water, and bathing containers elevated.

Living Conditions: Robust, but sensitive to cold, damp weather. Also bathes in damp leaves. Clean floor covering and furnishings every day or two. Mating pair should be able to select each other in flock. Freestanding nest in undergrowth; nesting aid: nesting basket; nest materials: grasses, plant fibers, moss, roots, cotton. Four eggs, incubation 12–13 days.

Social Behaviors: Incompatible with other Black-chinned Yuhinas; may be kept with other bird species.

Diet: Fine soft foods, fruits and berries, nectar drink, live food.

QUICK INFO **Order:** *Sparrows* **Family:** *Babblers* (→ p. 14)
Distribution: *From Himalayas to northern Myanmar and southeastern and southwestern China, South Vietnam.*

Black-headed Caique

Pionites melanocephala

Description: Males and females look the same; juveniles not as brightly colored. Shrill voice, loud in groups. Not strong fliers.

Housing: Cage or indoor aviary (24×24×32 in.); outdoor aviary (8×3×6 ft. at least 50°F / 10°C). Fresh branches for perching and gnawing; hard chewer.

Living Conditions: Enjoys bathing; rolling in wet leaves. Provide food and water containers off the ground. Nest box (10×10×20 in.); two to four eggs, incubation 26 days.

Social Behaviors: Active, playful, curious; sometimes aggressive, especially during breeding season. Behavior can be unpredictable.

Diet: Seed mixture for large parakeets, manufactured diets, fresh fruits and vegetables, tree buds, sprouted seeds; benefits from mineral supplements.

Housing:
Degree of Difficulty: 2
Voice:
Size: 9 in.

QUICK INFO Order: *Parrots* Family: *Parrots* (→ p. 6)
Distribution: *Colombia, Peru, Venezuela, the Guyanas.*

Black-headed Canary

Serinus alario

Also: *Alario alario*

Description: Female more uniform in color than male. Warbling song similar to that of canaries. Open nester.

Housing: Cage or indoor aviary (32×16×16 in.). Low bushes or small potted evergreens; attach twigs to cage bars. Floor surface, sand or concrete with good drainage. Provide containers with forest dirt. Place containers for food, drinking water, and bathing on ground.

Living Conditions: Keep cooler in winter. When kept in cages, tends toward weight gain, so provide plenty of free flight. Mating pair should be able to select each other in flock. Freestanding nest in vegetation or among twigs; nesting aids: nesting basket, commercially produced nest, half-open nesting box; nest materials: grasses, plant fibers, flock, moss, animal hairs. Three to five eggs, incubation 13 days.

Social Behaviors: Peaceable. Can be kept with other birds of its species and other small birds.

Diet: Seeds containing oils and carbohydrates (→ p. 246). Seeds of weeds and grasses, foxtail millet, sprouted food, green food, apples, and berries; grit in limited amounts.

Housing: 🏠 🏡
Degree of Difficulty: 2
Voice: 🎵
Size: 4½ –5 in.

QUICK INFO **Order:** *Sparrows* **Family:** *Finches* (→ p. 17) **Distribution:** *Southern and southwestern Africa.*

45

Black-headed Greenfinch

Carduelis ambigua

Also: *Chloris ambigua*

Description: Female like male, except gray head. Warbling, ringing song. Open nester.

Housing: Cage or indoor aviary (32×16×16 in.) or outdoor aviary with shelter (3×3 ft., no cooler than 50°F / 10°C). Evergreen plants for vegetation. Floor sand with good drainage. Food, water, and bathing containers on ground.

Living Conditions: Shy for a long time; needs vegetation for cover. Freestanding nest in evergreen tree; nesting aids: nesting block, commercially manufactured nest, nesting basket, hidden among twigs; nest materials: dried grasses, twigs, coconut fibers, sticks, flock, plant and animal wool. Three to five eggs, incubation 13–15 days. Successful breeding attempts.

Social Behaviors: Cantankerous during mating season. At other times may be kept with finches.

Diet: Small seeds containing carbohydrates and mainly oils (→ p. 246), weed and grass seeds, foxtail millet, sprouted food, green food, fruits and berries, fresh twigs with buds, live food; grit in limited amounts.

Housing:
Degree of Difficulty: 2
Voice:
Size: 5–5½ in.

QUICK INFO **Order:** *Sparrows* **Family:** *Finches* (→ p. 17) **Distribution:** *Southern Tibet to Indochina, western and southwestern China.*

Black-Rumped Waxbill

Estrilda troglodytes

Housing:	🔲 🏠 🏢
Degree of Difficulty: 1	
Voice:	♩
Size: 3½ –4 in.	

Description: Male and female look the same. Nest host of the Pintail Whydah (→ p. 159). Buzzing song; females sing also. Like to fly. Lively. Open nester.

Housing: Cage or indoor aviary (48×20×20 in., no cooler than 59°F / 15°C in summer or 65°F / 18°C in winter). Thick vegetation, floor sand or concrete; good drainage. Place food, water, and bathing containers on ground.

Living Conditions: Twelve- to fourteen-hour days with aid of light. Cylindrical nest usually on the ground in thick underbrush. Nesting aids: bags of heather among branches, half-open nesting boxes; nest materials: fine grass, bast, coconut fibers, plant wool, and feathers. Three to five eggs, incubation 12–14 days.

Social Behaviors: Peaceable. May be kept with other Black-rumped Waxbills and other Estrildid Finches.

Diet: Small-grained varieties of millet, canary grass seed, Niger seed, foxtail millet, sprouted food, half-ripe weed and grass seeds, green food, little live food; grit in limited quantities.

QUICK INFO **Order:** *Sparrows* **Family:** *Estrildidae (Waxbills and allies)* (→ p. 18) **Distribution:** Senegal to Ethiopia, south to Uganda.

Black and White Mannikin

Lonchura bicolor

Also: *Spermestes bicolor*

Description: Male and female look the same. Quiet, whistling, twittering song. Open nester.

Housing: Cage or indoor aviary (32×16×16 in.) or outdoor aviary with shelter (3×3 ft., no cooler than 65°F / 18°C). Thick vegetation. Floor sand with good drainage. Place food, water, and bathing containers close to ground level.

Living Conditions: Twelve- to fourteen-hour day with aid of light. Likes to bathe. Breeding successful only if mating pair can choose one another in the flock. Roundish nest in undergrowth; nesting aids: half-open nesting box, commercially manufactured nest; nest materials: coconut fibers, blades of grass, panicum. Three to six eggs, incubation 11–13 days.

Social Behaviors: During mating season, male often incompatible with other Mannikins and other finches; keep mating pair by themselves. Sociable at other times.

Diet: Small- and large-grained types of millet, reed canary grass seed, soaked wheat and oats, foxtail millet, sprouted food, green food; grit in limited amounts.

Housing:
Degree of Difficulty: 1
Voice: ♬
Size: 3¾–4 in.

QUICK INFO Order: *Sparrows* **Family:** *Estrildidae (Waxbills and allies)* (→ *p. 18*) **Distribution:** *From Gambia in the west to Cameroon and Kenya and on the east coast down to South Africa.*

Blue-cheeked Rosella

Platycercus adscitus

Housing:
Degree of Difficulty: 1
Voice:
Size: 12 in.

Description: Female the same color as the male, but with a smaller head. Metallic-sounding call in flight. Lively, good flier. Cavity nester.

Housing: Indoor aviary (6×3×3 ft., wire thickness ¹⁄₁₆ in.) or outdoor aviary with shelter (3×3 ft., no cooler than 50°F / 10°C). Natural wood branches for perching and climbing with sand underneath; free flying space. Provide opportunities to keep occupied (→ p. 242). Keep food, drinking water, and bathing containers slightly elevated.

Living Conditions: Enjoys bathing. Nesting cavities in nesting box (10–12×10–12×24 in., entry hole 3 in.); provide decayed wood. Three to five eggs, incubation 19–20 days. Brooding is not easy, for the male is often aggressive toward the female.

Social Behaviors: Keep mating pair by themselves: not compatible with other birds of the same or related species, even in a neighboring aviary.

Diet: Seed mixture for large parakeets, manufactured diets, (→ p. 246), foxtail millet, sprout food, grass and weed seeds, green food, fruit, and berries; grit; twigs for gnawing.

QUICK INFO Order: *Parrots* Family: *Parrots* (→ p. 6)
Distribution: *Eastern Australia from the Cape York Peninsula into northern New South Wales.*

Blue-faced Parrot Finch

Erythrura trichroa

Also: *Amblynura trichroa*

Description: Female same color as male, but less blue. Several color varieties possible. Song consists of warbling call. Open nester.

Housing: Indoor aviary (48×20×20 in.) or outdoor aviary with shelter (3×3 ft., no cooler than 61°F / 16°C; approximately 72°F / 22°C or heater for nesting box during breeding season). Vegetation, including bushes. Floor clean sand or concrete. Keep food, water, and bathing containers elevated.

Living Conditions: Twelve- to fourteen-hour day with aid of light. At night keep night-light on. Likes to bathe. Large nest in large or half-open nesting box (6×6×6 in.); nest materials: grasses, plant fibers, stalks. Separate breeding pair after mating season. Five to six eggs, incubation 13–14 days.

Social Behaviors: Peaceable. May be kept with other birds of its own species and other finches.

Diet: Small- and large-grained varieties of millet, canary grass seed, soaked wheat and oats, foxtail millet, sprouted food, weed and grass seeds, green food; grit in limited amounts.

Housing: 🏠 🏢
Degree of Difficulty: 2
Voice: 🎵
Size: 4¾ in.

QUICK INFO *Order:* Sparrows **Family:** *Finches* (→ p. 17) **Distribution:** *Sulawesi, Moluccas, New Guinea, Melanesia, Cape York Peninsula.*

Blue Front Amazon

Amazona aestiva

Housing:	🏠 📊
Degree of Difficulty: 1	
Voice: 🔊	
Size: 14½ in.	

Description: Male and female look the same. Loud cry; good mimic. Cavity nester.

Housing: All-metal indoor or outdoor aviary (6×3×3 ft., wire thickness ¾ in.) with shelter (3×3 ft., no cooler than 50°F / 10°C), shower installation. Floor concrete. Branches for perching and climbing; opportunities to keep occupied (→ p. 242). Keep food, water, and bathing containers elevated.

Living Conditions: Spray two to three times a week for high humidity. Mating pair should be able to select each other in flock. Cavity in nesting box (14×14×24–32 in., entry hole 4¾ in.). Resents nest checks, even aggressive toward caregiver during mating season. Usually three eggs, incubation 23–25 days.

Social Behaviors: Single bird needs bond with family; several birds may be kept together in aviary.

Diet: Seed mixture for Amazons, manufactured diets (→ p. 246), sprouted food, half-ripe seeds, green food, fruits and vegetables; twigs with buds for gnawing.

QUICK INFO **Order:** *Parrots* **Family:** *Parrots* (→ p. 6) **Distribution:** *Central Brazil, Paraguay, eastern Bolivia, northern Argentina.*

Blue and Gold Macaw

Ara ararauna

Also: Gold-breasted Macaw

Description: Male and female look the same. Yellow color (Golden Macaw) is available. Very loud voice; good imitator. Friendly. Cavity nester.

Housing: All-metal indoor or outdoor aviary (12×6×6 ft., wire thickness ¼₄ in.) with shelter (3×6 ft., at least 50°F / 10°C) and sprinkler installation. Floor of hard dirt, preferably concrete; good drainage. Natural wood branches for climbing and perching; provide something to keep birds occupied (→ p. 242) and a bowl with sand for bathing. Keep food, water, and bathing containers elevated.

Living Conditions: Spray every day. Hole in natural tree trunk or hardwood box (20×20×44 in., entry hole 6 in.); provide decayed wood for floor. Two to three eggs, incubation 25–30 days.

Social Behaviors: Keep one bird that's bonded with the family, or one pair.

Diet: Seed mixture for large parrots, manufactured diets, (→ p. 246), half-ripe sprouts, whole grains, live food, fruit, berries, green food; twigs to gnaw.

Housing: 🏠 🏞
Degree of Difficulty: 2
Voice: 🔊
Size: 34 in.

QUICK INFO Order: *Parrots* Family: *Parrots* (→ p. 6)
Distribution: *Eastern Panama to Bolivia, Paraguay, and Sao Paulo.*

Blue-gray Tanager

Thraupis episcopus

Housing: 🏠 🏢
Degree of Difficulty: 2
Voice: 🎵
Size: 6–7 in.

Description: Female the same color as the male, but more greenish. Song is a squeaking chirp. Very lively. Open nester.

Housing: Indoor aviary 48×20×20 in. or outdoor aviary with a shelter (3×3 ft., no cooler than 59–72°F / 15–20°C). Lots of plants, with shrubs or berry bushes. Dirt or concrete floor. Keep food, drinking water, and bathing containers elevated.

Living Conditions: Robust but sensitive to rain and draft. Likes to bathe. Clean floor every day or two. Freestanding nest in vegetation; nesting aids: half-open nesting box, nesting basket; nest materials: grass, fine twigs, leaves, moss. Two to three eggs, incubation 13–14 days. Many successful breeding attempts.

Social Behaviors: Doesn't get along with other birds of its own or related species, sometimes not even with other small birds, so keep mating pair by themselves.

Diet: Fruit, berries, vegetables, soft foods, live food, nectar drink.

QUICK INFO **Order:** *Sparrows* **Family:** *Buntings* (→ p. 15) **Distribution:** *Mexico to Peru and northwest Brazil, also on Trinidad and Tobago.*

Blue-headed Pionus

Pionus menstruus

Also: Red-vented Parrot

Description: Males and females look the same; juveniles have paler colors on head. Cavity brooders. Moderately noisy; not hard chewers.

Housing: Cage or indoor aviary (22×28×15 in.); outdoor aviary (8½×3×6 ft., at least 41°F / 5°C) with bare floor or concrete with good drainage. Provide food and water containers off the ground. Add perches, swings.

Living Conditions: Sometimes more receptive to showers than bathing. Breeds regularly. Provide wooden nest box (12×12×24 in., entry hole 4 in.) with pine shavings. Three to four eggs; incubation 26 days.

Social Behaviors: Gentle, sometimes shy or moody. Cautious. Easily stressed in new situations.

Diet: Seed mixture for large parrots, manufactured diets, fruits and vegetables, nuts, sprouts, nutritional supplements.

Housing: 🖼 🖼 🖼
Degree of Difficulty: 2
Voice: 🔊
Size: 11 in.

QUICK INFO **Order:** *Parrots* **Family:** *Parrots* (→ p. 6)
Distribution: *Bolivia, Brazil, Colombia, Costa Rica, Ecuador, Mexico, Peru.*

Blue-winged Leafbird

Chloropsis cochinchinensis

Housing: ⊞ 🏛 🏚
Degree of Difficulty: 2
Voice: 🎵
Size: 7 in.

Description: Female not as brightly colored as the male, with no black mask. Warbling song, good mimic; females also sing. Can quickly become friendly. Open nester.

Housing: Box cage / indoor aviary (48×24×36 in.) or outdoor aviary with shelter (3×3 ft., no cooler than 68°F / 20°C). Leave open flying room. Absorbent floor covering (birdcage litter), provide clean sand in bowl. Keep food, drinking water, and bathing containers elevated.

Living Conditions: Enjoys bathing in most leaves. Clean floor and furnishings every day or two. Bowl-shaped nest in thick vegetation; nesting aids: half-open nesting box; nest materials: soft grasses, fine roots. Two to three eggs, incubation 13–14 days.

Social Behaviors: Sometimes incompatible with other birds during mating season. May be kept together with small birds.

Diet: Soft food, egg food, live food, fruit, and berries with a little cracker, nectar drink, green food.

QUICK INFO Order: *Sparrows* Family: *Bluebirds (→ p. 12)* Distribution: *Sri Lanka, India to southwestern China, Southeast Asia south to Java, Borneo, and Sumatra.*

Bourke's Parrot

Neopsephotus bourkii

Housing: 🏠 🏠 🏠
Degree of Difficulty: 1
Voice: 🎵
Size: 7½ in.

Description: Female the same color as the male, but usually without blue on forehead, and without pink on belly. Various colors possible. Twittering voice. Good flier. Cavity nester.

Housing: Cage / indoor aviary (36×18×18 in.) or outdoor aviary, wire thickness ¹⁄₁₆ in. with shelter (3×3 ft., no cooler than 50°F / 10°C) and sprinkler. Floor surface sand or concrete; good drainage. Doesn't gnaw, so plants are possible, but keep flying room clear. Natural wood branches for perching and climbing. Place food and water containers near ground level.

Living Conditions: Let caged birds exercise outside of cage. Rain or spray bath. Nesting box (6–8×6–8×10–14 in., entry hole 1½ –2½ in.); nesting material: wood shavings. Provide several nesting possibilities; the bird will choose. Three to six eggs, incubation 18 days.

Social Behaviors: May be kept with others of its kind or small birds.

Diet: Seed mixture for parakeets, manufactured diets, (→ p. 246), foxtail millet, sprout food, half-ripe grass and weed seeds, green food, fruit; grit; twigs to gnaw.

QUICK INFO Order: *Parrots* Family: *Parrots* (→ p. 6)
Distribution: *Dry regions of southern Australia.*

Brahminy Starling

Sturnus pagodarum

Also: *Temenuchus pagodarum*
Description: Male and female look the same. Melodious, whistling song; good imitator. Playful and lively. Cavity nester.

Housing: Cage or indoor aviary (48×24×36 in.) or sheltered upright outdoor aviary with shelter (6×3 ft., no cooler than 59–64°F / 15–18°C). Abundant vegetation. Floor, birdcage litter. Place food, water, and bathing containers on ground.

Living Conditions: Robust bird species. Likes plenty of sun and water baths. Clean or change floor covering and furnishings every day or two. Mating pair should be able to choose each other in flock. Nest in natural tree trunk or half-open nesting box (8×8×12 in.); lots of nest materials: grasses, dead leaves, moss, animal hair, feathers. Three to fi eggs, incubation 12–14 days.

Social Behaviors: May be kept with other Brahminy St and fairly large bird species, but not with smaller spec

Diet: Fruits and berries, coarse soft food containing i live food, diced meat, green food.

Housing:
Degree of Difficulty: 1
Voice:
Size: 8–9 in.

QUICK INFO Order: *Sparrows* **Family:** *Starlin*
Distribution: *Sri Lanka, India, Nepal, eastern Afg*

Bronze Mannikin

Lonchura cucullata

Description: Both sexes similar in appearance. Soft, quick twittering song. Nest sleeper. Open nester.

Housing: Indoor aviary (32 × 16 × 16 in., no cooler than 59°F / 15°C), vegetation of bushes or branches attached to grating. Ground cover sand with good drainage. Place food, water, and bathing containers near ground level.

Living Conditions: Undemanding, fairly robust. Twelve- to fourteen-hour day with aid of light. Likes to bathe. Mating pair should be able to select each other from flock. Nest in undergrowth; nesting aids: nesting basket, half-open or closed nesting box (1½–2 in. entry hole); nesting materials: coconut and sisal fibers, soft grasses and feathers. Four to six eggs, incubation 12–13 days. Frequently successful breeding attempts.

Social Behaviors: Male sometimes cantankerous during breeding season, so keep mating pair by themselves. Peaceable other times.

small- and large-grained varieties of millet, canary grass seed, ed wheat and oats, foxtail millet, sprouted food, grass seeds, green food; grit in limited amounts.

INFO Order: *Sparrows* **Family:** *Estrildidae (Waxbills → p. 18)* **Distribution:** *All of Africa south of the to the southwest.*

Housing:
Degree of Difficulty: 1
Voice:
Size: 3½ in.

Bronze-winged Pionus

Pionus chalcopterus

Also: Bronze-winged Parrot

Description: Males and females look
the same. Congregates in flocks. Swift,
agile fliers.

Housing: 🔲 🏠 🏢
Degree of Difficulty: 2
Voice: 🔊
Size: 11 in.

Housing: Cage or indoor aviary (22×28×15 in.); outdoor
aviary (8½×3×6 ft., at least 41°F / 5°C) with bare floor and
good drainage. Provide food and water containers off the
ground. Add perches, swings.

Living Conditions: Sometimes more receptive to showers
than bathing. Breeds regularly. Provide wooden nest box
(12×12×24 in., entry hole, 4 in.) with pine shavings. Four to
five eggs, incubation 26–28 days.

Social Behavior: Gentle, sometimes shy or moody. Cautious.
Easily stressed in new situations.

Diet: Seed mixture for large parrots, manufactured diets,
fruits and vegetables, nuts, sprouts, nutritional suppleme

QUICK INFO **Order:** *Parrots* **Family:** *Parrots (—*
Distribution: *Andes of Colombia, Ecuador, Peru, V*

Budgerigar

Melopsittacus undulatus

Description: Male with blue cere, female cere with beige to brown waxy skin. Various colors possible. Warbling, twittering voice. Becomes friendly. Good flier. Cavity nester.

Housing: Cage or indoor aviary (36×18×18 in.) or outdoor aviary (wire thickness ¹⁄₁₆ in.) with frost-free shelter (36×18 in.). Floor sand or concrete. Natural branches for perching and climbing; leave flying room open; provide something to keep birds busy (→ p. 242). Place food, water, and bathing containers on ground.

Living Conditions: Easy keeper. Likes to bathe. At least two hours of free flight per day for cage-kept birds. Nesting cavity nesting box (7×7×10 in.). Four to six eggs, incubation 18 s. Reliable nester.

Behaviors: Very sociable, so keep at least a pair—better hole flock.

d mixture for parakeets (→ p. 246), sprouted food, uit, vegetables, green food; fresh twigs for gnawing; ; offer manufactured diet.

Housing:
Degree of Difficulty: 1*
Voice:
Size: 7–9½ in.

IFO Order: *Parrots* **Family:** *Parrots* (→ p. 6) Central Australia.

California Quail

Callipepla californica

Housing:
Degree of Difficulty: 1
Voice: ♩
Size: 9–10 in.

Description: Female less brightly colored than male, without black on head. Digs on the ground for food. Sleeps in trees. Ground nester.

Housing: Indoor or partly covered, draft-free outdoor aviary (6×3×6 ft.) with shelter (3×3 ft., no cooler than 50°F / 10°C). Thick vegetation; leave open floor space. Floor dirt; bowl with sand for sand bath. Perching branches high in shelter for sleeping place, sheltered by evergreen branches. Place food, water, and bathing containers on ground.

Living Conditions: Sensitive to moisture. Change sand every one to two days. Nest hidden in hollow on ground, lined with leaves and stems. Ten to seventeen eggs, incubation 22–23 days.

Social Behaviors: May be kept with tree-dwelling birds, but not with gallinaceous birds.

Diet: Mixture of seeds containing carbohydrates and a little oil (→ p. 246), weed and grass seeds, foxtail millet, sprouted food, green food, live food, grit.

QUICK INFO **Order:** *Gallinaceous Birds* **Family:** *Gallinaceans* (→ *p. 6*) **Distribution:** *American West Coast, naturalized in Hawaii, New Zealand, Chile, Argentina.*

Canary

Serinus serinus

Housing: 🏠 🏢
Degree of Difficulty: 1
Voice: 🎵
Size: 4¼–4¾ in.

Description: Female less brightly colored than the male. Song: quick, squeaking twitter at the same pitch; persistent singer. Can become friendly. Open nester.

Housing: Indoor (32×16×16 in.) or outdoor aviary with frost-free shelter (3×3 ft.). Thick vegetation including bushes. Floor sand with good drainage. Keep food, water, and bathing containers elevated.

Living Conditions: Undemanding. Remains shy in cage. Bowl-shaped nest freestanding in vegetation; nesting aids: nesting block, commercially manufactured nest, provided with twigs; nest materials: plant and root fibers, lichens, moss, flock, and soft, dry grasses. Three to four eggs, incubation 13 days. Reliable breeders.

Social Behaviors: Argumentative during breeding season; afterwards may be kept with other finches.

Diet: Seeds containing oils and carbohydrates (→ p. 246), weed and grass seeds, foxtail millet, sprouted food, green food, fruits and berries, live food, fresh twigs with buds; grit in limited amounts.

QUICK INFO Order: *Sparrows* Family: *Finches* (→ p. 17) Distribution: *Central Europe, Mediterranean Region, eastward to Baltic.*

Canary-winged Parrot

Brotogeris versicolurus

Housing:	
Degree of Difficulty: 1	
Voice:	
Size: 8¾ in.	

Description: Male and female look the same. Often shrill, metallic cries; mating pair call out in duet. The photo shows the Canary-winged Parrot (*Brotogeris versicolurus chiriri*).

Housing: Indoor or outdoor aviary (36×18×18 in., wire thickness ¾ in.) with shelter (18×36 in., no cooler than 59°F / 15°C). Floor sand. Provide branches for perching and climbing. Keep food, water, and bathing containers elevated.

Living Conditions: Robust, undemanding species. Likes to bathe. Mating pair should be able to select each other in flock. Nesting cavity in nesting box (8×8×16 in., entry hole 2½ in.); put in a thick layer of peat moss or decayed wood. Three to five eggs, incubation approximately 26 days.

Social Behaviors: May be kept with small birds, and with other Canary-winged Parrots only in a large aviary.

Diet: Seed mixture for large parakeets, manufactured diets (→ p. 246), sprouted food, grass seeds, green food, vegetables, fruits, berries; twigs for gnawing.

QUICK INFO Order: *Parrots* Family: *Parrots (→ p. 6)*
Distribution: *Amazon basin from French Guyana to southeastern Colombia and northeastern Peru.*

Cape Canary

Serinus canicollis

Also: Graynecked Canary

Description: Female the same color as the male, but not as bright. Warbling song. Open nester.

Housing: Indoor (32×16×16 in.) or outdoor aviary with shelter (3×3 ft., no cooler than 50°F / 10°C). Thick vegetation. Floor sand with good drainage. Place food, water, and bathing containers close to ground level.

Living Conditions: Robust birds, but protect against dampness. Easily gain weight when kept in a cage, so provide opportunities for free flight. Nest in vegetation; nesting aids: nesting basket, commercially manufactured nest; nest materials: plant and animal wool, sisal and coconut fibers, grasses, roots. Three to five eggs, incubation 14 days. Breeding attempts successful.

Social Behaviors: Argumentative during mating season; after that time, may be kept with other finches.

Diet: Seeds containing oils and carbohydrates (→ p. 246); ripe and half-ripe seeds from trees, weeds, and grasses; foxtail millet; plenty of sprouted food, green food; apples and berries; live food; grit in limited amounts.

Housing:

Degree of Difficulty: 2

Voice:

Size: 5 in.

QUICK INFO Order: *Sparrows* **Family:** *Finches* (→ *p. 17*)
Distribution: *Ethiopia along the Great Rift Valley to Cape Province, Angola.*

Cape Dove

Oena capensis

Housing: 📦 📦
Degree of Difficulty: 1
Voice: ♩
Size: 10¼–11 in.

Description: Female the same color as the male, but without black mask. Tail 4½–5¼ in. long. Friendly. Open nester.

Housing: Indoor aviary or sheltered vertical outdoor aviary (9×5×6 ft.) with shelter (6×3 ft., no cooler than 68°F / 20°C). Thick vegetation, but leave open area on floor. Floor sand; bowl with fine sand for bath. Place food, water, and bathing containers on floor.

Living Conditions: Needs warmth. Protect from cold, damp weather. Loose nest; nesting aids: commercially manufactured nest, half-open nesting box (4×4×4 in.) with pre-made nest of varying height on wall or in undergrowth. Two eggs, incubation 13–16 days. Easy but unreliable breeders.

Social Behaviors: Occasionally incompatible with other doves and species of doves during mating season. May be kept with other bird species.

Diet: Seed mixture for parakeets (→ p. 246), small sunflower seeds, sprouted or soaked seeds, green food; grit in limited amounts.

QUICK INFO **Order:** *Doves* **Family:** *Doves* (→ p. 6)
Distribution: *Southwestern Arabia, Africa south of the Sahara, Madagascar.*

Cape Siskin

Serinus tottus

Also: *Pseudochloroptila totta*

Description: Female the same color as the male, but more subdued and with more pronounced streaking. Warbling, trilling song. Not too skittish. Open nester.

Housing: Cage or indoor aviary (32×16×16 in.) or outdoor aviary with shelter (3×3 ft., no cooler than 59°F / 15°C). Plantings with bushes, but leave open areas. Floor sand with good drainage. Place food, water, and bathing containers near ground level.

Living Conditions: Easy keepers, but need warmth. Provide nesting aid (nesting basket) high in aviary; nest materials: grasses, plant and root fibers, coconut and sisal fibers, plant and animal wool, flock. Three to four eggs, incubation 16–17 days. Successful breeding attempts.

Social Behaviors: Peaceable. May be kept with other Cape Siskins and other small birds.

Diet: Seeds containing oils and carbohydrates (→ p. 246), weed and grass seeds, foxtail millet, sprouted food, green food, fruits and berries, live food, fresh twigs with buds; grit in limited amounts.

Housing: 🖿 🏠 🏚
Degree of Difficulty: 1
Voice: 🎵
Size: 4¾–5 in.

QUICK INFO **Order:** *Sparrows* **Family:** *Finches (→ p. 17)* **Distribution:** *Southern and southwestern Cape Province.*

Chaffinch

Fringilla coelebs

Housing:
Degree of Difficulty: 1
Voice: ♫
Size: 5½–6 in.

Description: Female browner than male. Various colors possible. Melodic, warbling song. Open nester.

Housing: Indoor aviary (48×20×20 in.) or outdoor aviary with frost-free shelter (3×3 ft.). Vegetation, including bushes and evergreens. Floor sand or concrete; good drainage. Place food, water, and bathing containers on ground.

Living Conditions: Robust, likes to bathe. Bowl-shaped nest freestanding in vegetation. Nesting aids: nesting blocks, commercially manufactured nest, nesting basket, nesting box disguised with twigs; nest materials: coconut fiber, flock, small feathers, root fibers, animal hair, moss. Three to six eggs. Incubation 12–13 days. Frequently successful breeding attempts.

Social Behaviors: During breeding season aggressive toward other birds, so keep breeding pair by themselves. At other times may be kept with other chaffinches and small birds.

Diet: Seeds containing oils and carbohydrates (→ p. 246), weed and grass seeds, foxtail millet, sprouts and green foods, apples, berries, live food; twigs with buds.

QUICK INFO **Order:** *Sparrows* **Family:** *Finches* (→ *p. 17*)
Distribution: *Europe (up to the far north) to Western Siberia, around the Mediterranean, Asia Minor, and Near East to Trans-Caspian Region.*

Chattering Lory

Lorius garrulus

Housing: 🏠
Degree of Difficulty: 2
Voice: 🔊
Size: 12 in.

Description: Female the same color as the male, but brighter yellow neck spot, usually smaller. Loud screech, chortling sounds; good imitator. May become friendly. Cavity nester.

Housing: All-metal outdoor aviary (6×3×3 ft., wire thickness ¹⁄₁₆ in.) with shelter (3×3 ft., no cooler than 50°F /10°C). Vegetation consisting of blooming bushes. Floor 6 inches of coarse gravel or concrete. Natural branches for perching and climbing; opportunities to keep occupied (→ p. 242). Keep food, water, and bathing containers elevated.

Living Conditions: Likes to bathe. Clean floor and furnishings daily. Nesting cavity in natural tree trunk or nesting box (8×8×24 in., entry hole 3½–4 in.), put in 4–6 in. decayed wood or wood shavings. Two eggs, incubation 26–28 days.

Social Behaviors: May be kept with fairly large birds from other species as long as no cavity nesters are included.

Diet: Lori soup (→ p. 249); pollen; soft fruits; carbohydrate-rich seeds such as millet, oats, and wheat; sprouted food; live food; twigs with buds.

QUICK INFO **Order:** *Parrots* **Family:** *Parrots* (→ p. 6)
Distribution: *Moluccas.*

Cherry Finch

Aidemosyne modesta

Housing:
Degree of Difficulty: 2
Voice: ♩
Size: 4–4½ in.

Description: Female same color as the male, but without black on the throat and between eye and upper beak; diagonal striping more crooked. Very soft, twittering, warbling song. Can become friendly. Open nester.

Housing: Indoor aviary (32×16×16 in.) or outdoor aviary with shelter (3×3 ft., no cooler than 64–68°F / 18–20°C). Vegetation consisting of bushes, grass, and reeds. Floor sand with good drainage. Food, water, and bathing containers near ground level.

Living Conditions: Sensitive to cold and dampness. Twelve- to fourteen-hour day with aid of light. Cage is not appropriate: birds can become overweight. Regularly check claws. Mating pair should be able to select each other in flock. Nest in vegetation; nesting aids: nesting box; nest materials: grasses, coconut and sisal fibers, raffia. Frequent nest checks. Four to five eggs, incubation 13 days. Reliable nesters.

Social Behaviors: Aggressive toward other Cherry Finches. May be kept with other Estrildidae.

Diet: Small- and large-grained varieties of millet; canary grass seed; Niger seed; foxtail millet; ripe, half-ripe, and sprouted weed and grass seeds; green food; grit in small amounts.

QUICK INFO **Order:** *Sparrows* **Family:** *Estrildidae (Waxbills and allies) (→ p. 18)* **Distribution:** *Eastern Australia.*

Cherry-headed Conure

Aratinga erythrogenys

Also: Red-masked Conure

Description: Male and female look the same; juveniles green with no red feathers. Loud voice. Strong fliers.

Housing: Cage or indoor aviary (24×24×48 in.); outdoor aviary with shelter (9×3×6 ft.); keep from frost. Provide food, water, and bathing containers off the floor. Natural branches for perching and climbing.

Living Conditions: Likes to bathe. Sometimes reluctant to breed. Provide wooden nest box (10×10×20 in., entry hole 2½ in.). Three to four eggs, incubation 23 days.

Social Behavior: Sometimes shy and cautious. Once familiar with others, enjoys playful interaction.

Diet: Seed mixture for large parakeets, manufactured diets, fresh fruits and vegetables, wild greens, nuts, sprouts. Mineral, vitamin, calcium supplements; rearing foods, bread, when raising young.

Housing:
Degree of Difficulty: 2
Voice:
Size: 13 in.

QUICK INFO Order: *Parrots* **Family:** *Parrots* (→ p. 6)
Distribution: *Colombia, Ecuador, Peru, Venezuela.*

Chestnut Breasted Mannikin

Lonchura castaneothorax

Housing:
Degree of Difficulty: 1
Voice:
Size: 3¾–4¼ in.

Also: *Munia castaneothorax*

Description: Female similar to male, but not as brightly colored. Song: rasping, twittering. Lively. Open nester.

Housing: Cage / indoor aviary (32×16×16 in.) or outdoor aviary with shelter (3×3 ft., no cooler than 65°F / 18°C). Vegetation of tall grass or reeds and bushes. Floor sand or concrete with good drainage. Place food, water, and bathing containers near ground.

Living Conditions: Robust species. Provide twelve- to fourteen-hour day with aid of light. Cage-kept birds may gain weight, so allow free flight. Nest in vegetation; nesting aids: half-open nesting box, nesting blocks; nest materials: grasses, plant wool, plant fibers. Four to six eggs, incubation approximately 13 days.

Social Behaviors: Peaceable. Several pairs and other finches can be kept together.

Diet: Small- and large-grained varieties of millet, canary grass seeds, soaked wheat and oats, foxtail millet, sprouted food, weed and grass seeds, green food; grit in limited amounts.

QUICK INFO **Order:** *Sparrows* **Family:** Estrildidae (Waxbills and allies) (→ p. 18) **Distribution:** *Northern and southeastern New Guinea, northwestern and eastern Australia, New Caledonia, New Hebrides.*

Chestnut Munia

Lonchura Malacca

Also: *Munia Malacca*

Description: Female not as brightly colored as the male. Photo (L to R): Chestnut Munia, White-haired Munia, White-capped Munia (*Lonchura ferruginosa*). Open nester.

Housing: Indoor aviary (32×16×16 in., no cooler than 64°F / 18°C). Vegetation consisting of grass, reeds, and shrubbery. Floor sand with good drainage. Place food, water, and bathing containers near ground level.

Living Conditions: Undemanding, robust. Twelve- to fourteen-hour day with aid of light. Check claws regularly. Mating pair should be able to select each other in flock. Spherical nest in undergrowth, or nesting basket or half-open nesting box; nest materials: grasses, plant fibers, hairs. Four to six eggs, incubation 14–15 days. Reliable nester.

Social Behaviors: Several mating pairs may be kept together and with other Estrildidae.

Diet: Small varieties of millet, canary grass seed, foxtail millet, half-ripe and sprouted weed and grass seeds, green food; limited amounts of grit.

Housing: 🏠
Degree of Difficulty: 1
Voice: ♩
Size: 4½–4¾ in.

QUICK INFO Order: *Sparrows* **Family:** *Estrildidae (Waxbills and allies) (→ p. 18)* **Distribution:** *Southern India, Sri Lanka (Three-colored Munia), eastern Nepal to western Myanmar (Black-headed Munia), Java, and Bali (White-capped Munia).*

Chinese Painted Quail

Coturnix chinensis

Housing:
Degree of Difficulty: 1
Voice: ♩
Size: $4\frac{3}{4}$–$5\frac{3}{4}$ in.

Also: Chinese Button Quail, Blue-breasted Quail
Description: Female has no black-and-white chin and throat markings. Various colors possible. Deep, three-syllable crowing. Lively.
Housing: Cage or indoor aviary (48×24×36 in.) with sand floor; soft roof to prevent injuries if birds become frightened and fly upward. Outdoor aviary (6×3×6 ft.) with frost-free shelter (3×3 ft.). Part of aviary floor covered with dirt, vegetation of grass and bushes; other part, open floor for digging. Bowl with fine sand for sand bath. Food, water, and bathing containers on ground.
Living Conditions: Robust bird species. Best to keep one male with three to four females. Nest a flat hollow in the ground under bushes. Four to eight eggs, incubation 16–18 days. Reliable nesters.
Social Behaviors: May be kept with other brush dwellers, but no other ground dwellers.
Diet: Mixture of seeds containing carbohydrates and oils (→ p. 246), foxtail millet, green food; grit and cuttlebone.

QUICK INFO **Order:** *Gallinaceans* **Family:** *Gallinaceans (→ p. 6)* **Distribution:** *India to southeast Asia, Indonesia, Philippines and New Guinea to Northern Australia.*

Cobalt-winged Parakeet

Brotogeris cyanoptera

Housing: ⊞ ⊡
Degree of Difficulty: 2
Voice: ♩
Size: 7 in.

Description: Females have less yellow on heads; juveniles have darker heads and bills. Fast fliers, noisy in groups. Roosts in treetops; avoids ground. Not hard chewers.

Housing: Cage or indoor aviary (48×16×20 in.); outside aviary (7½×3×6 ft., at least 41°F / 5°C). Fresh tree branches. Provide food and water containers off the ground.

Living Conditions: Enjoys bathing, showers. Cavity nesters. Need Budgerigar-sized wooden nest boxes, or block of decaying wood or rotted tree stump to excavate own nesting site. Three to eight eggs; incubation 23 days.

Social Behaviors: Lively in groups, seldom aggressive to other Brotogeris species; single birds quiet, gentle.

Diet: Seed mixture for parakeets, manufactured diets, fresh fruits and vegetables, wild greens; supplemental vitamins beneficial.

QUICK INFO Order: *Parrots* **Family:** *Parrots (→ p. 6)* **Distribution:** *Brazil, Bolivia, Colombia, Ecuador, Mexico, Peru, Venezuela.*

Cockatiel

Nymphicus hollandicus

Housing: [icons]
Degree of Difficulty: 1*
Voice: [icon]
Size: 12½–13 in.

Description: Red ear patch is brighter in males than in females. Several colors possible. Melodic, rhythmic whistle; good mimic. Can become friendly. Cavity nester.

Housing: Cage or indoor aviary or outdoor aviary (6×3×3 ft., wire thickness ⅛ in.) with frost-free shelter (3×3 ft.). Floor sand or concrete. Branches for perching and climbing; opportunities to keep occupied (→ p. 242). Keep food, water, and bathing containers elevated.

Living Conditions: Robust species. If kept in a cage, allow daily free flight. Cavity in nesting box or natural tree trunk (12×12×14–16 in., entry hole 3¾ in.); climbing aid inside, put in wood shavings. May resent nest check. Four to six eggs, incubation 18–21 days.

Social Behaviors: Keep mating pair by themselves during breeding season. At other times may be kept with other seed eaters.

Diet: Seed mixture for cockatoos; offer manufactured diet (→ p. 246); sprouted food, fruits, vegetables, green food; softwood branches for gnawing.

QUICK INFO **Order:** *Parrots* **Family:** *Cockatoos* (→ p. 7)
Distribution: *Interior of Australia.*

Common Bullfinch

Pyrrhula pyrrhula

Housing:
Degree of Difficulty: 1
Voice:
Size: 6–6½ in.

Description: Female the same color as the male, but underside beige-gray. Chatty, warbling, whistling song; females also sing. Open nester.

Housing: Cage or indoor aviary (48×20×20 in.) or outdoor aviary with frost-free shelter (3×3 ft.). Vegetation with robust bushes such as elder, arborvitae, and holly (they love it!). Floor sand with good drainage. Keep food, water, and bathing containers elevated.

Living Conditions: Easy keepers. Mating pair should be able to select one another in flock. Bowl-shaped nest in vegetation; nesting aids: nesting basket, nesting block, commercially manufactured nest; nest materials: roots, moss, animal hair, feathers, grasses. Four to six eggs, incubation approximately 14 days.

Social Behaviors: Argumentative during mating season; thereafter may be kept with other finches.

Diet: Small seeds containing carbohydrates and mainly oils (→ p. 246), weed and grass seeds, foxtail millet, sprouted food, green food, fruits and berries, fresh twigs with buds, live food; grit in limited amounts.

QUICK INFO Order: *Sparrows* Family: *Finches (→ p. 17)* Distribution: *Eurasia from northern Spain to Japan.*

Common Canary

Serinus canaria

Description: Bred as varieties for song, color, posture, and conformation. Size varies according to breed. Melodic warbling, whistling song. Can become friendly. Open nester.

Housing: Depending on breed, cage or indoor aviary (32–64× 16–32×16–32 in.) or outdoor aviary with frost-free shelter (3 ×3 ft.). Vegetation and perches, but without reducing flying room. Floor sand with good drainage. Place food, water, and bathing containers near ground level.

Living Conditions: Undemanding, robust. Likes to bathe. Daily free flight for birds kept in cages. Nest in undergrowth or concealed by twigs; nesting aids: nesting basket, half-open nesting box; nest materials: grasses, flock, plant fibers. Four eggs, incubation 13–14 days.

Social Behaviors: Peaceable. May be kept with other canaries and other small birds.

Diet: Canary food mixture consisting of canary grass seed, foxtail millet, hemp or rape seeds, green food, vegetables, fruits and berries, fresh twigs with buds and leaves; cuttlebone and grit in limited amounts.

Housing: 🔲 🏠 🗄
Degree of Difficulty: 1*
Voice: 🎵
Size: 4½–9 in.

QUICK INFO **Order:** *Sparrows* **Family:** *Finches* (→ p. 17)
Distribution: *Original form lives on Canary Islands, the Azores, Madeira.*

Common Hill Mynah

Gracula religiosa

Housing: ▦ ▣ ⛶
Degree of Difficulty: 2
Voice: ♫ ◖))
Size: 9–14 in.

Description: Male and female look the same. Sonorous call; good imitators. Can become very friendly. Like exercise. Produce lots of runny droppings. Sleep in cavities. Cavity nester.

Housing: Box cage / indoor aviary (48×24×36 in.) with strong wire mesh or an outdoor aviary with a shelter (6×3 ft., no cooler than 50°F / 10°C). Sleeping box inside shelter. Absorbent floor covering (birdcage litter or newspaper). Keep food, water, and bathing containers elevated, secure firmly.

Living Conditions: When kept in cage, at least two hours of free flight a day. Likes to bathe. Change floor covering every day or two. Intolerant to dampness and cold. Mating pair should be able to select each other in flock. Nesting cavities in nesting box or natural tree trunk (10×10×16–20 in., entry hole 4 in.); nest materials: leaves, hay, coconut fibers, feathers. Two to three eggs, incubation approximately 15 days.

Social Behaviors: May be kept with other birds of the same and different species in a large aviary.

Diet: Special food for mynahs or coarse soft food, fruits, and berries.

QUICK INFO Order: *Sparrows* Family: *Starlings* (→ p. 21) Distribution: *Sri Lanka, India to Malaysia, and Indonesia.*

Common Mynah

Acridotheres tristis

Housing: 🏠 🏞
Degree of Difficulty: 2
Voice: 🎵
Size: 8¾–9 in.

Description: Male and female look the same. Loud, warbling, melodic song, squeaking call; good imitator. Lively and curious. Cavity nester.

Housing: Indoor aviary (48×24×36 in.) or outdoor aviary with shelter (3×3 ft., no cooler than 68°F / 20°C). Thick vegetation. Floor birdcage litter. Food, water, and bathing containers on ground.

Living Conditions: Gains weight if it doesn't get exercise. Clean or change floor covering and furnishings every day or two. Repeated successful breeding attempts. Mating pair should be able to select each other from among flock. Nest in nesting box or hollowed-out tree trunk, fairly high in aviary; nest materials: grasses, leaves, and twigs. Four to five eggs, incubation 14–18 days.

Social Behaviors: Argumentative during breeding season; keep mating pair alone during that time. Otherwise, may be kept with other Mynahs and larger bird species.

Diet: Fruits and berries, coarse soft foods containing insects, live food, small pieces of meat, green food. Dietary supplements—speak with an avian veterinarian.

QUICK INFO Order: *Sparrows* **Family:** *Starlings* (→ p. 21)
Distribution: *Afghanistan and Iran through India to Indochina.*

Common Rosefinch

Carpodacus erythrinus

Also: *Erythrina erythrina*

Description: Mature males mostly red and brown, younger males colored like females, without red hues. Soft, whistling song. Open nester.

Housing: Cage or indoor aviary (40×20×20 in.) or outdoor aviary with shelter (3×3 ft., no cooler than 59°F / 15°C). Thick vegetation, floor cover sand with good drainage. Keep food, water, and bathing containers elevated.

Living Conditions: Sensitive to cold. Nest in undergrowth; nesting aids: nesting basket, half-open nesting box; nest materials: coconut fibers, grasses, thin twigs. Four to five eggs, incubation 12–14 days. Successful breeding attempts.

Social Behaviors: Aggressive toward other Common Rosefinches and similarly colored birds during mating season. Peaceable at other times.

Diet: Small seeds containing carbohydrates and mainly oils (→ p. 246), weed and grass seeds, foxtail millet, sprouted food, green food, fruits and berries, fresh twigs with buds, live food; grit in limited amounts.

Housing: ▦ ▣ ▦
Degree of Difficulty: 2
Voice: ♫
Size: 5½–6 in.

QUICK INFO Order: *Sparrows* **Family:** *Finches (→ p. 17)*
Distribution: *Middle, eastern, and northern Europe as far as Kamchatka, Caucasus through Himalayas to middle China.*

Common Waxbill

Estrilda astrild

Housing: 🏠 🏢
Degree of Difficulty: 1
Voice: 🎵
Size: 4–4¾ in.

Description: Female less brightly colored than male. Song a loud twittering, warbling, scratching. Lively; likes to climb. Open nester.

Housing: Indoor aviary (32×16×16 in.) or outdoor aviary with shelter (3×3 ft., no cooler than 59°F / 15°C). Thick vegetation of bushes, small trees, and tufts of grass; large open space for flying, ground cover sand; provide bowl with sprouted grass seeds. Place food, water, and bathing containers near ground level.

Living Conditions: Twelve- to fourteen-hour day with aid of light. Spherical nest freestanding in vegetation; nesting aid: nesting basket; nest materials: fine grass stalks, coconut and sisal fibers, wool, hairs, feathers. Sensitive to nest checks. Four to six eggs, incubation 12–13 days. Nesting quite frequently successful.

Social Behaviors: May be kept with other Common Waxbills and other Estrildidae.

Diet: Small-grained varieties of millet; canary grass seed; foxtail millet; ripe, half-ripe, and sprouted weed and grass seeds; green food; live food; grit in limited amounts.

QUICK INFO **Order:** *Sparrows* **Family:** *Estrildidae (Waxbills and allies)* (→ p. 18) **Distribution:** *Nearly all of Africa south of the Sahara.*

81

Crimson-breasted Bluebill

Spermophaga haematina

Housing: 🏠 🏢
Degree of Difficulty: 2
Voice: 🎵
Size: 5½ in.

Description: Male black and red, female more likely dark brown. Whistling, trilling, warbling, squeaking song. Can become friendly. Lively. Open nester.

Housing: Indoor aviary (40×20×20 in.) or outdoor aviary with shelter (3×3 ft., no cooler than 72°F / 22°C, approximately 83°F / 28°C for raising young). Thick vegetation consisting of bushes and grasses. Floor sand with good drainage. Place food, water, and bathing containers near ground level.

Living Conditions: Undemanding. Twelve- to fourteen-hour day with aid of light. Freestanding nest in undergrowth; nesting aids: half-open nesting box; nest materials: grasses, coconut fibers, leaves. Often resent nest checks. Four eggs, incubation 15–18 days. Breeding attempts often successful.

Social Behaviors: Aggressive toward other Crimson-breasted Bluebills and related species during mating season; peaceable toward other Estrildidae.

Diet: Small-grained varieties of millet (despite their hefty beak), canary grass seed, foxtail millet, sprouted food, half-ripe and ripe weed and grass seeds, green food, live food; grit, healing earth, a little charcoal.

QUICK INFO **Order:** *Sparrows* **Family:** *Estrildidae (Waxbills and allies)* (→ p. 18) **Distribution:** *Western Africa.*

Crimson Finch

Neochmia phaeton

Description: Female the same color as the male, but with less red. Resonant, trilling voice. Very lively. Likes to climb in underbrush, flies a lot. Open nester.

Housing:		
Degree of Difficulty: 3		
Voice:	♫	
Size: 4½–5½ in.		

Housing: Indoor aviary (48×20×20 in.) or outdoor aviary with shelter (3×3 ft., no cooler than 68°F / 20°C). Thick vegetation consisting of bamboo, reeds, and shrubs, but don't restrict flying room. Floor sand; provide good drainage. Keep food, water, and bathing containers elevated.

Living Conditions: Sensitive to damp and cold. Twelve- to fourteen-hour day with aid of light. Freestanding nest in vegetation or in half-cavity nesting box; nest materials: plant fibers, corn leaves, raffia, small white feathers, and plant wool. Five to six eggs, incubation 12–14 days.

Social Behaviors: Keep mating pair by themselves at all times because of their aggressiveness, even toward larger birds.

Diet: Small- and large-grained varieties of millet; canary grass seed; foxtail millet; ripe, half-ripe, and sprouted weed and grass seeds; green food; live food; small amounts of grit.

QUICK INFO **Order:** *Sparrows* **Family:** *Estrildidae (Waxbills and allies)* (→ p. 18) **Distribution:** *Northern Australia, southern New Guinea.*

Crimson Rosella

Platycercus elegans

Housing: 🏠 🏤
Degree of Difficulty: 1
Voice: 🎵
Size: 13–14 in.

Description: Male and female look the same, but female is slightly smaller. Several colors possible. Chattering voice. Likes to fly; spends lots of time on ground. Cavity nester.

Housing: Indoor or outdoor aviary (6×3×3 ft., wire thickness ⁵⁄₆₄ in.) with frost-free shelter (3×3 ft., warm in the case of *P.e. nigrescens*). Concrete floor, but sand under branches used for perching and climbing. Opportunities to keep occupied (→ p. 242). Keep food, water, and bathing containers on ground.

Living Conditions: Hardy. Likes to bathe. Change sand every two to three days; check regularly for worms. Nesting cavity in a long box (12×12×39 in., entry hole 3½–4 in.), climbing aid inside for female and young birds; put in a little sawdust. Four to six eggs, incubation 19–21 days.

Social Behaviors: Keep mating pair by themselves: incompatible with other Crimson Rosellas and related species, even in neighboring aviary.

Diet: Seed mixture for large parakeets (→ p. 246), foxtail millet, sprouted food, weed and grass seeds, green food, fruits and berries; twigs for gnawing; offer manufactured diet.

QUICK INFO **Order:** *Parrots* **Family:** *Parrots* (→ p. 6)
Distribution: *Southeastern and eastern Australia.*

Crimson-rumped Waxbill

Estrilda rhodopyga

Housing: 🔲 🏠 🏢
Degree of Difficulty: 1
Voice: ♩
Size: 4–4½ in.

Description: Female the same color as the male, but not as bright. Song a series of nasal calls. Likes to fly. Open nester.
Housing: Cage or indoor aviary (32×16×16 in.) or outdoor aviary with shelter (3×3 ft., no cooler than 68°F / 20°C). Thick vegetation of bushes and grass or branches for perching; leave flying room. Floor sand with good drainage. Place food, water, and bathing containers near ground level.
Living Conditions: Robust species. Twelve- to fourteen-hour day with aid of light. Mating pair should be able to select each other in flock. Covered nest freestanding in vegetation; nesting aids: half-open nesting box, commercially manufactured nest, parakeet box; nest materials: coarse and fine grasses, sisal and coconut fibers, small feathers, dirt. Four to five eggs, incubation 12–13 days.
Social Behaviors: May be kept with other Crimson-rumped Waxbills and other Estrildidae.
Diet: Small- and large-grained varieties of millet, canary grass seed, soaked wheat and oats, foxtail millet, sprouted food, weed and grass seeds, green food; grit in limited amounts.
QUICK INFO **Order:** *Sparrows* **Family:** *Estrildidae (Waxbills and allies)* (→ p. 18) **Distribution:** *Sudan, Eritrea to northern Mozambique and as far as the western shore of Lake Albert.*

Crimson-winged Parakeet

Aprosmictus erythropterus

Description: Male with orange-red, female with light brown iris; female less brightly colored than male. Likes to fly. Cavity nester.

Housing: Outdoor aviary (6×3×3 ft., wire thickness 5/64 in.) with frost-free shelter (3×3 ft.) and shower setup. Floor sand or concrete. Provide branches for perching and climbing, and ways to keep busy. Food, water, and bathing containers near ground level.

Living Conditions: Sensitive to temperature. Likes to bathe. Cavity in natural tree trunk or nesting box (10–12× 10–12×24 in., entry hole 4–5 in.), provide climbing aids on inner wall, put in some decayed wood. Five to six eggs, incubation 20–21 days.

Social Behaviors: Aggressive toward other Crimson-winged Parakeets and related species, even in neighboring aviary. May be kept with seed eaters.

Diet: Seed mixture for large parakeets, manufactured diets (→ p. 246), foxtail millet, sprouted food, ripe and half-ripe grass seeds, ripe and half-ripe corncobs, fruits and berries, vegetables, green food; twigs for gnawing.

Housing:
Degree of Difficulty: 2
Voice: ♩
Size: 12½–13 in.

QUICK INFO Order: *Parrots* Family: *Parrots* (→ p. 6)
Distribution: *Northern and eastern Australia, New Guinea.*

Cut-throat Finch

Amadina Fasciata

Housing: 🎴 🎴 🎴
Degree of Difficulty: 1
Voice: 🎵
Size: approximately 5 in.

Description: Female lighter in color than male, without red throat band. Different colorations possible. Humming, buzzing song. Lively. Sleeps in nest. Half-cavity nester.

Housing: Cage or indoor aviary (32×16×16 in.) or protected outdoor aviary with shelter (3×3 ft., no cooler than 64°F / 18°C). Provide thick vegetation. Floor surface sand with good drainage. Place food, drinking water, and bathing containers on floor.

Living Conditions: Twelve to fourteen hours' daylight with aid of light. Slight weight gain when kept in cage. Allow free flight. Prepared nest in closed or half-open nesting box (5×5×6 in.); additional nesting materials: grasses, coconut and sisal fibers, raffia, feathers. Four to six eggs, incubation 12–14 days.

Social Behaviors: Keep pair alone during breeding time; take over nests of other inhabitants. Other than during breeding time, may be kept with other types of birds.

Diet: Small- and large-grained varieties of millet, canary grass seeds, soaked wheat and oats, foxtail millet, sprouted food, weed and grass seeds, green food; grit in limited quantities.

QUICK INFO **Order:** *Sparrows* **Family:** *Estrildidae (Waxbills and allies)* (→ p. 18) **Distribution:** *Senegal to eastern Ethiopia, Somalia, south as far as Mozambique, Zimbabwe, and Botswana.*

Dark Firefinch

Lagonosticta rubricata

Also: *Dunkelroter Amarant*

Housing: [icons]
Degree of Difficulty: 2
Voice: [icon]
Size: 4½ in.

Description: Female similar to male, but not as brightly colored. Melodic, warbling, trilling, twittering, meowing song. Many different calls. Open nester.

Housing: Outdoor aviary (6×3×3 ft.) with shelter (3×3 ft., no cooler than 68°F / 20°C). Keep in indoor aviary (32×16×16 in.) during winter. Bushes or twigs for cover, open floor surface for dust baths. Floor clean sand with good drainage. Place food, water, and bathing containers on ground.

Living Conditions: Needs warmth. Twelve- to fourteen-hour day with aid of light. In cage, remains shy and skittish. Likes to bathe. Freestanding nest in undergrowth; nesting aids: nesting basket; nest materials: dried grass, coconut and sisal fibers. Three to five eggs, incubation 11–13 days.

Social Behaviors: May be kept with other Dark Firefinches and other finches.

Diet: Small and large-grained types of millet, canary grass seed, soaked wheat and oats, foxtail millet, sprout food, weed and grass seeds, green food; grit in limited amounts.

QUICK INFO Order: *Sparrows* Family: *Finches (→ p. 17)* Distribution: *Western, eastern, and southern Africa.*

Diamond Dove

Geopelia cuneata

Also: *Stictopeleia cuneata*

Description: Female same color as the male, but eye ring is not quite as red. Several colors possible. Voice gentle cooing, soft howl. Quickly becomes friendly. Stays on ground. Open nester.

Housing: 🔲 🏠 🏢
Degree of Difficulty: 1
Voice: ♩
Size: 7½–9½ in.

Housing: Cage or indoor aviary (48×24×36 in.) or outdoor aviary with a frost-free shelter (3×3 ft.). Vegetation, including bushes. Floor dirt; provide a bowl with sand for bathing. Place food, water, and bathing containers on the ground.

Living Conditions: Undemanding. Quite hardy. Likes to take sun and shower baths. Nests in nesting box (5×5×7 in.), basket, or open box in underbrush; nest materials: grasses, twigs, coconut fibers. Two eggs, incubation 13 days. Breeding attempts frequently successful.

Social Behaviors: During breeding season sometimes incompatible with other Diamond Doves. May be kept with other bird species such as finches.

Diet: Mix of seeds containing carbohydrates and oils (→ p. 246), weed seeds, sprout food, green food, ant larvae, and a little soft food; grit; offer dietary supplements.

QUICK INFO   Order: *Doves* **Family:** *Doves* (→ p. 6)
Distribution: *Australia, except for south.*

Diamond Firetail Finch

Emblema guttata

Also: *Stagonopleura guttata*

Description: Male gray, red, black, and white; female similar to male, but smaller. Deep, humming song, high, whistling call. Open nester.

Housing:		
Degree of Difficulty: 1		
Voice: ♩		
Size: 4½–4¾ in.		

Housing: Indoor aviary (48×20×20 in.) or outdoor aviary with shelter (3×3 ft., no cooler than 50°F / 10°C). Bushes, but open ground area. Floor sand or concrete with good drainage. Place food, water, and bathing containers close to ground level.

Living Conditions: Twelve- to fourteen-hour day with aid of light. Likes to bathe. Easily gains weight when kept in a cage. Mating pair should be able to select each other in flock. Large freestanding nest in underbrush; nesting aids: large nesting box (7×7×10 in.); nest materials: grasses, plant wool, feathers, plant fibers. Usually five eggs, incubation 14 days. Regular breeders.

Social Behaviors: Male generally very aggressive with birds that have red markings, so keep mating pair by themselves.

Diet: Small- and large-grained varieties of millet, canary grass seed, soaked wheat and oats, foxtail millet, sprouted food, weed and grass seeds, green food; grit in limited amounts.

QUICK INFO **Order:** *Sparrows* **Family:** *Finches* (→ p. 17) **Distribution:** *Southern and southeastern Australia.*

Double-barred Finch

Poephila bichenovii

Also: *Stizoptera bichenovii*

Description: Male and female look the same. Song rarely heard. Can become friendly. Lively, like to climb in branches. Open nester.

Housing: Cage or indoor aviary (32×16×16 in.) or outdoor aviary with shelter (3×3 ft., no cooler than 68°F / 20°C). Thick vegetation of bushes and shrubs. Floor sand, areas with grasses, good drainage. Place food, water, and bathing containers on ground.

Living Conditions: Twelve- to fourteen-hour day with aid of light. Mating pair should be able to select each other in flock. Freestanding nest in undergrowth; nesting aids: nesting basket or half-open box (4×4 in.) behind a few branches; nest materials: coconut and sisal fibers, grass stalks. Four to seven eggs, incubation 12–14 days. Reliable nesters.

Social Behaviors: May be kept with several mating pairs and other Estrildidae species.

Diet: Small-grained varieties of millet, canary grass seed, foxtail millet, half-ripe and sprouted weed and grass seeds, green food, live food; grit in limited quantities.

Housing:

Degree of Difficulty: 1

Voice: ♩

Size: 4 in.

QUICK INFO **Order:** *Sparrows* **Family:** *Estrildidae (Waxbills and allies)* (→ p. 18) **Distribution:** *Northern and southern Australia.*

Double Yellow-headed Amazon

Amazona o. oratrix

Housing: 🏚 🏠 🏘
Degree of Difficulty: 2
Voice: 🔊
Size: 15 in.

Description: Males may have more yellow than females. Strong fliers. Loud, forceful voice. Hard chewer. Active; enjoys climbing. Cavity brooders.

Housing: Cage or indoor aviary (30×30×36 in.) or outdoor aviary (12×4½×6 ft.) with shelter (4½×3×6 ft., at least 50°F / 10°C). Provide food, water, and bathing containers off the floor. Natural branches for climbing and perching.

Living Conditions: Likes to bathe. Requires regular supply of wood for chewing. Nesting box (12×12×20 in.); two to four eggs; incubation 26 days.

Social Behaviors: Friendly, playful. Becomes extremely aggressive to keeper while breeding.

Diet: Seed mixture for Amazons, manufactured diets, fruits and vegetables, sprouts, wild greens, mineral supplements.

QUICK INFO Order: *Parrots* **Family:** *Parrots* (→ p. 6)
Distribution: *Mexico.*

Dusky Pionus

Pionus fuscus

Also: Dusky Parrot

Description: Male and female look the same. Cavity brooders. Moderately noisy; not hard chewers.

Housing: Cage or indoor aviary (22×28×15 in.); outdoor aviary (7½×3×6 ft., at least 50°F / 10°C) with bare floor and good drainage. Provide food and water containers off the ground. Perches, swings.

Living Conditions: Sometimes more receptive to showers than bathing. May be reluctant to breed; provide wooden nest box (12×12×24 in., entry hole 4 in.) with pine shavings. Three to four eggs; incubation 26 days.

Social Behaviors: Gentle, sometimes shy or moody; may not be compatible with other parrots. Cautious; sometimes stressed in new situations.

Diet: Seed mixture for large parrots, manufactured diets, fruits and vegetables, nuts, sprouts, nutritional supplements.

Housing: 🔲 🔲 🔲
Degree of Difficulty: 2
Voice: 🔊
Size: 10¼ in.

QUICK INFO **Order:** *Parrots (Psittaciformes)* **Family:** *Parrots (Psittacidae) (→ p. 6)* **Distribution:** *Brazil, Colombia, Guyana.*

Dybowski Twinspot

Euschistospiza dybowskii

Housing: 🎴 🏛

Degree of Difficulty: 2

Voice: 🎵

Size: 4¼–4¾ in.

Description: Female similar to male, but lighter in color. Melodious, twittering, warbling, trilling song; females sing also. Can become friendly. Open nester.

Housing: Cage or indoor aviary (32×16×16 in.). Large-leaf vegetation; provide twigs on cage mesh. Floor sand; clean with good drainage. Place food, water, and bathing containers near ground level.

Living Conditions: Twelve- to fourteen-hour day with aid of light. Mating pair should be able to select each other in flock. Freestanding nest in vegetation; nesting aids: nesting basket with coconut-fiber cushion, nesting box; nest materials: dried grass, coconut fibers, moss, hair, flock, feathers. Four to five eggs, incubation 13–14 days.

Social Behaviors: Male generally very aggressive, especially with others of its species or other red birds.

Diet: Small- and large-grained varieties of millet, canary grass seed, soaked wheat and oats, foxtail millet, sprouted food, weed and grass seeds, green food; grit in limited quantities.

QUICK INFO Order: *Sparrows* **Family:** *Estrildidae (Waxbills and allies)* (→ *p. 18*) **Distribution:** *Senegal and Sierra Leone to the Congo, Sudan to Central Africa.*

Eclectus Parrot

Eclectus roratus

Housing: 🏠 🏢
Degree of Difficulty: 2
Voice: 🎵
Size: 14–17 in.

Description: Female predominantly red and purplish blue, male green. Sonorous voice. Can become friendly. Cavity nester.

Housing: All-metal indoor or outdoor aviary (9×3×6 ft.; mesh size 8×8 in., wire thickness ¾ in.) with shelter (6×3 ft., no cooler than 59°F / 15°C). Floor concrete with good drainage. Branches for perching and climbing; leave room for flying; provide opportunities to keep occupied (→ p. 242). Keep food, water, and bathing containers elevated.

Living Conditions: Likes to bathe. Provide large nesting boxes (12–14×24×12–14 in., entry hole 4–5 in.). One to two eggs, incubation 26–28 days.

Social Behaviors: Female dominant and aggressive toward her male and other females. During breeding season, keep mating pair by themselves.

Diet: Seed mixture for large parrots, manufactured diets (→ p. 246), foxtail millet, sprouted food, soft food containing insects, nuts, fruits, berries, carrots and corn to meet high Vitamin A requirement; fresh twigs for gnawing.

QUICK INFO **Order:** *Parrots* **Family:** *Parrots* (→ p. 6)
Distribution: *Moluccas, Lesser Sunda Islands, New Guinea and surrounding islands, northern Australia.*

Elegant Parrot

Neophema elegans

Also: Blue-winged Parrot

Description: Female less brightly colored than the male, without red belly spot. Several colors possible. Melodious twittering. Cavity nester.

Housing: Housing: Degree of Difficulty: 2 Voice: Size: 9 in.

Housing: Indoor or outdoor aviary (36×18×18 in., wire thickness ¾₄ in.) with shelter (36×18 in., no cooler than 64°F / 18°C). Sparse vegetation, open, ground covered with short grass. Branches for perching and climbing. Keep food, water, and bathing containers elevated.

Living Conditions: Protect from cold and damp. Nesting cavity in natural tree trunk or nesting box (8×8×12 in., entry hole 1½–2½ in.); put in a little sawdust or peat moss; nest materials: small grass stems. Four to six eggs, incubation 18–19 days.

Social Behaviors: Aggressive toward other Elegant Parrots or related species, even in neighboring aviary. May be kept with Estrildidae, doves, or chickens.

Diet: Seed mixture for large parakeets, manufactured diets (→ p. 246), foxtail millet, sprouted food, seed containing only a little oil, green food, fruits and vegetables; fresh twigs for gnawing.

QUICK INFO Order: *Parrots* Family: *Parrots* (→ p. 6)
Distribution: *Southeastern and southwestern Australia.*

European Goldfinch

Carduelis carduelis

Also: Goldfinch

Housing:
Degree of Difficulty: 1
Voice:
Size: 5½ in.

Description: Female the same color as the male, but the red face marking is smaller. Various colors possible. Song consists of twittering, warbling sequence. Can become friendly. Open nester.

Housing: Indoor cage (32×16×16 in.) or outdoor aviary with frost-free shelter (3×3 ft.). Vegetation of bushes such as elder, privet, or arborvitae. Floor sand with good drainage. Place food, water, and bathing containers near ground level.

Living Conditions: Robust species. Bowl-shaped nest freestanding in vegetation; nesting aids: nesting block, nesting basket, commercially manufactured nest; nest materials: soft plant fibers, grasses, fine roots and moss. Four to six eggs, incubation 12–14 days. Breeding attempts frequently successful.

Social Behaviors: May be kept with other European Finches and other finches in a large aviary.

Diet: Small seeds containing oils and a little carbohydrate (→ p. 246), weed and grass seeds, foxtail millet, sprouted food, green food, berries, live food; small amounts of grit.

QUICK INFO **Order:** *Sparrows* **Family:** *Finches (→ p. 17)* **Distribution:** *Europe except for northern, North Africa, large part of Asia.*

European Robin

Erithacus rubecula

Description: Male and female look the same. Melodious, effervescent, melancholy, warbling song audible all year long. Can become friendly. Lively. Open nester.

Housing: Outdoor aviary (6×3×6 ft.) with frost-free shelter (3×3 ft.). Floor dirt with roots, piles of twigs. With mating pairs, subdivide with thick vegetation or twigs, and provide several feeding places. Place food, water, and bathing containers on ground.

Living Conditions: A robust species. Birds adjust quickly. Undemanding. Nest well camouflaged on ground; nesting aids: half cavities, commercially manufactured nest; nesting materials: dried leaves, grasses, moss, plant fibers, plant wool. Four to six eggs, incubation 13–15 days.

Social Behaviors: Incompatible with other European Robins, some females, and other red-colored species. May be kept with species that aren't red.

Diet: Soft food containing insects, live food; also red and blue berries and grapes in the fall.

Housing: [icon]
Degree of Difficulty: 1
Voice: [icon]
Size: 5–5½ in.

QUICK INFO **Order:** *Sparrows* **Family:** *Thrushes* (→ p. 13)
Distribution: *Europe even in the far north, northern Africa, Azores, Canary Islands, east to western Siberia, the Caucasus, northern Iran.*

Fairy Bluebird

Irena puella

Housing:	🏠 🏢
Degree of Difficulty: 2	
Voice:	🎵
Size: 10½–11½ in.	

Description: Female the same color as the male, but more greenish turquoise. Warbling song, soft chattering. Can become friendly. Likes to fly. Open nester.

Housing: Indoor aviary (6×3×6 ft.), in summer also outdoor aviary with shelter (3×3 ft., no cooler than 64°F / 18°C). Thick vegetation; leave flying room. Absorbent floor covering; provide sand in bowls. Keep food, water, and bathing containers elevated.

Living Conditions: Keep indoors during winter; toes become frostbitten easily. Clean ground and furnishings every day or two. Flat nest freestanding in vegetation; nesting aids: nesting basket, half-open or open nesting box; nest materials: twigs, moss, grass, animal hair, fine roots. Two to three eggs, incubation 13 days.

Social Behaviors: Peaceable. May be kept with seed eaters such as Estrildidae or small doves, as well as with tanagers and nectar eaters.

Diet: Sweet fruits, nectar drink, soft food, egg food, green food; calcium supplements.

QUICK INFO **Order:** *Sparrows* **Family:** *Bluebirds* (→ p. 12) **Distribution:** *Southern India to Indochina, Indonesia, and the Philippines.*

Fischer's Lovebird

Agapornis fischeri

Housing:		
Degree of Difficulty: 1		
Voice:	🔊	
Size: 5¾–6 in.		

Description: Male and female look the same. Various colors possible. Shrill call, twitter. Cavity nester.

Housing: Cage or indoor aviary (36×18×18 in.) or outdoor aviary, wire thickness ¹⁄₁₆ in.) with frost-free shelter (3×3 ft.). Floor sand. Branches for perching and climbing; opportunities to keep occupied (→ p. 241). Food, water, and bathing containers near ground level.

Living Conditions: Hardy. Daily playtime outside of cage for birds kept in cages. Likes to bathe. Mating pair should be able to select one another in flock. Nesting cavity in nesting box (10×6×8 in., entry hole 2 in.); provide moist peat moss; nest materials: pieces of bark, twigs. Four to five eggs, incubation 22–23 days.

Social Behaviors: Flock may be kept in large aviary; keep mating pair by themselves in cage.

Diet: Seed mixture for parakeets (→ p. 246), foxtail millet, sprouted food, fruits, vegetables, green food; cuttlebone; twigs to chew apart; offer manufactured diet.

QUICK INFO **Order:** *Parrots* **Family:** *Parrots (→ p. 6)*
Distribution: *Originally only south and east of Victoria Sea, northwestern Tanzania as far as Burundi and Rwanda.*

Galah or Rose-breasted Cockatoo

Eolophus roseicapillus

Housing: ⊞ ⊞
Degree of Difficulty: 2
Voice:))))
Size: 13¾–14¼ in.

Description: Male darker brown, female has reddish-brown iris. Two-syllable metallic call; good mimic. Cavity nester.

Housing: All-metal indoor or outdoor aviary (6×3×3 ft., wire thickness ¹⁄₆₄–³⁄₃₂ in.) with shelter (3×3 ft., no cooler than 59°F / 15°C). Concrete floor with 6 in. of sand-dirt mixture. Branches for perching and climbing; leave space for flying; opportunities to keep occupied (→ p. 242). Keep food, water, and bathing containers on ground.

Living Conditions: Spray. With inadequate exercise, birds may gain weight. Change floor covering as needed. Check regularly for worms. Nesting cavity in natural tree trunk or nesting box (12–14×12–14×24–32 in., entry hole 4–4¾ in.). Two to five eggs, incubation 23–24 days.

Social Behaviors: During mating season, keep pair by themselves. Keep only single bird with parrots of same size.

Diet: Seed mixture for cockatoos (→ p. 246), sprouted food, fruits, vegetables, green food, softwood twigs for gnawing; offer manufactured diet.

QUICK INFO **Order:** *Parrots* **Family:** *Cockatoos* (→ p. 7) **Distribution:** *Australia.*

Goffin Cockatoo

Cacatua goffini

Description: Male has dark brown iris; female's is reddish-brown. Very noisy. Lively. Sleeps elevated. Likes to dig. Cavity nester.

Housing: All-metal indoor or draft-free outdoor aviary (6×3×3 ft.) with shelter (3×3 ft., no cooler than 59°F / 15°C) and sprinkler. Concrete floor with 6-in. mixture of sand and dirt. Branches for perching and climbing; provide things to keep birds occupied (→ p. 242); leave flying room. Attach food, water, and bathing containers to wall.

Living Conditions: Check for worms. Likes showers and spray baths (water 75–86°F / 24–30°C). Nesting cavity in tree trunk (inside diameter 12–14 in., 24–32 in. deep, entry hole 4–5 in.). Two to three eggs, incubation approximately 28 days.

Social Behaviors: During mating season keep mating pair by themselves. One bird can be kept with parrots of comparable size.

Diet: Seed mixture for cockatoos, manufactured diets (→ p. 246), sprouted food, fruits, vegetables, green food; softwood twigs for gnawing.

Housing: 🏠 🏚
Degree of Difficulty: 2
Voice: 🔊
Size: 12–13 in.

QUICK INFO **Order:** *Parrots* **Family:** *Cockatoos* (→ *p. 7*)
Distribution: *Tanimbar Islands (Indonesia).*

Golden-breasted Starling

Cosmopsarus regius

Description: Male and female look the same; tail up to 9½ in. long. Squawking or whistling call. Curious and lively. Can become friendly. Cavity nester.

Housing: Covered outdoor aviary (6×3×6 ft.) with shelter (6 ×3 ft., no cooler than 61°F / 16°C). Unsuited to indoor living because of possible unpleasant odors. Thick vegetation. Absorbent floor covering (birdcage litter or beech wood chips). Install food, water, and bathing containers near ground level or attach to wall.

Living Conditions: Likes to bathe. Clean or change floor covering and furnishings every day or two. Mating pair should be able to select each other from flock. Nest in roomy nesting box (12×12×24 in.). Resents nest checks. Two to four eggs, incubation 14 days. Numerous successful breeding attempts.

Social Behaviors: May be kept with other Golden-breasted Starlings and larger bird species, but not with smaller species.

Diet: Fruits and berries, coarse soft food containing insects, live food, diced meat, green food.

Housing:
Degree of Difficulty: 2
Voice:
Size: 13–14 in.

QUICK INFO Order: *Sparrows* Family: *Starlings* (→ p. 21)
Distribution: *Southern Ethiopia, Somalia, and Kenya to north-eastern Tanzania.*

Golden-fronted Leafbird

Chloropsis aurifrons

Housing: 🖼️ 🏠 🏡
Degree of Difficulty: 2
Voice: 🎵
Size: 7½–8 in.

Description: Female the same color as the male, but not as bright, with smaller throat patch. Melodic song, good mimic; females also sing. Open nester.

Housing: Cage or indoor aviary (48×24×36 in.) or outdoor aviary (6×3×6 ft.) with shelter (3×3 ft., no cooler than 68°F / 20°C). Thick vegetation with flowering bushes and bulb plants. Branches for perching and climbing. Absorbent floor covering, provide sand in bowls. Keep food, water, and bathing containers elevated.

Living Conditions: Intolerant of cold. Likes to bathe in damp leaves. Nest well hidden in underbrush; nesting aid: cross-section of evergreen tree trunk with branches; nesting material: long coconut and sisal fibers, bast. Two to three eggs, incubation 14–15 days. Breeding difficult because of male's aggressive disposition.

Social Behaviors: Occasionally argumentative with other Golden-fronted Leafbirds during mating season. May be kept with thrushes or tanagers in an aviary or alone in cage.

Diet: Large flakes of soft food, nectar drink, fruits and berries, live food.

QUICK INFO **Order:** *Sparrows* **Family:** *Bluebirds (→ p. 12)* **Distribution:** *India and Sri Lanka to southern China and Sumatra.*

Golden-mantled Rosella

Platycercus eximius

Housing:
Degree of Difficulty: 2
Voice:
Size: 12½–13½ in.

Description: Female the same color as the male; red on the breast is duller. Loud voice, rising scale, chortling and warbling. Very playful. Can become friendly. Lively, good flier. Cavity nester.

Housing: Indoor or outdoor aviary (6×3×3 ft., wire thickness 1⁄16 in.) with frost free shelter (3×3 ft.). Floor dirt, sand under perching and climbing branches; leave flying room; opportunities to keep occupied (→ p. 242). Food, water, and bathing containers on ground.

Living Conditions: Robust species. Reliable nester. Nesting hole in nesting box (10–12×10–12×24 in., entry hole 3¼ in.), provide wood shavings. Five to nine eggs, incubation 18–20 days.

Social Behaviors: Keep mating pair by themselves; incompatible with other Golden-mantled Rosellas and related species, even in neighboring aviary.

Diet: Seed mixture for large parakeets, manufactured diets (→ p. 246), foxtail millet, sprouted food, weed and grass seeds, green food, fruits and berries; twigs for gnawing.

QUICK INFO **Order:** *Parrots* **Family:** *Parrots (→ p. 6)*
Distribution: *Southeastern Australia (Victoria to southern Queensland), Tasmania; established in New Zealand.*

Golden Tanager

Tangara arthus

Housing: [icons]
Degree of Difficulty: 2
Voice: [icon]
Size: 5–5½ in.

Description: Female colored like male, but not as bright. Unremarkable song. Open nester.

Housing: Indoor aviary (32×16×16 in.) or outdoor aviary with shelter (3×3 ft., no cooler than 61°F / 15°C). Thick vegetation with berry-producing bushes. Absorbent floor covering (birdcage litter or beech wood chips). Keep food, water, and bathing containers elevated.

Living Conditions: Likes warmth. Change or clean floor covering and furnishings every day or two. Freestanding nest in undergrowth; nesting aids: half-open nesting box, nesting basket; nest materials: grass, thin twigs, leaves, moss. Two eggs, incubation 12–13 days. Fairly successful breeder.

Social Behaviors: During mating season, aggressive toward other Tanagers and other birds with similar colors. May be kept with other small birds except during mating season.

Diet: Fruits, berries, vegetables, soft food, live food, nectar drink; food containing carotene to retain bright coloration of plumage.

QUICK INFO **Order:** *Sparrows* **Family:** *Buntings* (→ p. 15) **Distribution:** *Venezuela and Colombia to northern Bolivia.*

Goldie's Lorikeet

Trichoglossus goldiei

Housing: 🏠 🏠 🏠
Degree of Difficulty: 2
Voice: ♩
Size: 7½ in.

Description: Male and female similar; male has more red feathers on the head; stronger violet color. Swift fliers; moves in flocks; can be screechy but generally pleasant sounding.

Housing: Cage or indoor aviary (18×18×24 in.) outdoor aviary (6×3×6 ft., at least 50°F / 10°C). Provide food and water containers off the floor; branches for chewing; swings for playing and perching; nest box for sleeping.

Living Conditions: Enjoys occasional showers. Provide wooden nest box (6×12×6 in.). One to two eggs, incubation 23 days.

Social Behaviors: Shy, startles easily; not aggressive. Does well in communities of similarly sized mixed species.

Diet: Commercially prepared lory diets, fresh fruits and vegetables, flowers. Offer calcium and mineral supplements.

QUICK INFO Order: *Psittaciformes* **Family:** *Loriidae* **Distribution:** *New Guinea.*

Gouldian Finch

Chloebia gouldiae

Housing: ⊞ 🏠 🏡
Degree of Difficulty: 1
Voice: 🎵
Size: 5–5½ in.

Description: Female colored like male, but not quite as bright. Several color variations possible. Song is an effervescent twittering. Lively. Open or cavity nester.

Housing: Cage or indoor aviary (48×20×20 in.) or outdoor aviary with shelter (3×3 ft., no cooler than 68°F / 20°C). Sparse vegetation. Floor sand or concrete; good drainage. Place food, water, and bathing containers close to ground level.

Living Conditions: Provide atmospheric humidity of 60–70% and twelve- to fourteen-hour day with the aid of a light. Mating pair should be able to select each other from flock. Nest in open basket, half-open or closed nesting box, oblong parakeet nesting box; nest materials: lots of plant fibers, soft grasses, moss. Three to eight eggs, incubation 14–15 days.

Social Behaviors: Peaceable. May be kept with several mating pairs and other Estrildidae finches.

Diet: Small- and large-grained varieties of millet, sprouted food, weed and grass seeds, green food; grit in limited amounts.

QUICK INFO Order: *Sparrows* **Family:** *Estrildidae (Waxbills and allies)* (→ p. 18) **Distribution:** *Northern Australia.*

Gray-headed Negrofinch

Nigrita canicapilla

Housing: 🏠 🏠
Degree of Difficulty: 2
Voice: ♩
Size: 5–5½ in.

Description: Male and female look the same. However, the female has a daintier beak. Soft, sonorous, whistling song. Lively behavior in the aviary. Open nester.

Housing: Indoor aviary (48×20×20 in.) or outdoor aviary with a shelter (3×3 ft., no cooler than 59°F / 15°C). Thick vegetation with robust plants (they love buds and blossoms!). Clean dirt or concrete floors; good drainage. Natural wood perches. Keep food and water containers elevated.

Living Conditions: Bathes in damp leaves. Twelve- to fourteen-hour day with aid of light. Easily gains weight when kept in cage. Large cylindrical nest in undergrowth; nesting aids: half-open nesting box, nesting basket; nest materials: coconut and sisal fibers, grasses, moss, panicum, plant and animal wool. Four to six eggs, incubation 12–13 days. Successful breeding attempts.

Social Behaviors: Aggressive toward other Gray-headed Negrofinches and related species, not with other Estrildidae.

Diet: Soft food containing insects, especially soft live food; egg food, nectar drink, fruit.

QUICK INFO **Order:** *Sparrows* **Family:** *Estrildidae (Waxbills and allies)* (→ p. 18) **Distribution:** *Sierra Leone east to Kenya, south to Angola.*

Gray Singer Finch

Serinus leucopygius

Also: White-rumped Seedeater,
Ochrospiza leucopygia

Housing:			
Degree of Difficulty: 1			
Voice: ♪			
Size: 4–4½ in.			

Description: Male and female look the same. Twittering, trilling song. Become friendly. Lively. Open nester.

Housing: Cage or indoor aviary (32×16×16 in.) or outdoor aviary with shelter (3×3 ft., no cooler than 50°F / 10°C). Thick vegetation. Floor sand with good drainage. Keep food, water, and bathing containers elevated.

Living Conditions: Undemanding. Freestanding nest in vegetation; nesting aids: nesting box, commercially manufactured nest, half-open nesting box; nest materials: plant fibers, sisal and coconut fibers, soft grasses, moss, small feathers, plant and animal wool. Three to four eggs, incubation 13 days. Reliable nester.

Social Behaviors: Aggressive during mating season; keep isolated during that time. Other times may be kept with finches.

Diet: Seeds containing oils and carbohydrates (→ p. 246), weed and grass seeds, foxtail millet, sprouted food, green food, fruits and berries, live food; grit in limited amounts.

QUICK INFO **Order:** *Sparrows* **Family:** *Finches (→ p. 17)*
Distribution: *Senegal and Gambia, across Mali to northern Ethiopia, Sudan, and northwestern Uganda.*

Green-cheeked Amazon

Amazona viridigenalis

Description: Female same color as the male, but the red on the top of the head is not as pronounced. Several possible colors. Shrill voice. Likes to climb. Cavity nester.

Housing: Outdoor aviary (6×3×3 ft., wire thickness ⅜ in.) with frost-free shelter (3×3 ft.) and sprinkler. Floor concrete. Hardwood perches and climbing branches; opportunities for activity (→ p. 242). Keep food, water, and bathing containers elevated.

Living Conditions: Easy to keep. Spray two to three times per week for humidity. Mating pair should be able to select each other in flock. Nesting cavity in hardwood nesting box or tree trunk (inside diameter 12–14 in., depth 24–32 in., entry hole 5 in.). Two to three eggs, incubation approximately 26 days.

Social Behaviors: Keep mating pair by themselves; incompatible with other Green-cheeked Amazons and other parrots, even in neighboring aviaries.

Diet: Seed mixture for Amazons, manufactured diets (→ p. 246), sprouted food, half-ripe seeds, green food, fruits and vegetables; twigs with buds for gnawing.

Housing:
Degree of Difficulty: 2
Voice:
Size: 13 in.

QUICK INFO **Order:** *Parrots* **Family:** *Parrots* (→ p. 6)
Distribution: *Northeastern Mexico.*

Green-cheeked Conure

Pyrrhura molinae

Description: Male and female look the same. Quick, strong fliers. Quiet voice. Lively, social, friendly. Several colors possible.

Housing: Cage or indoor aviary (18×18×24 in.); outdoor aviary (9×3×6 ft., nest box to protect from cold). Provide food, water, and bathing containers off the ground. Branches for perching and climbing; nest boxes for sleeping.

Living Conditions: Frequent bather. Eager breeder. Wooden nest box (10×10×10 in.). House breeding pairs separately or the hens will lay eggs in the same box. Three to seven eggs; incubation 23 days.

Social Behaviors: Bold, sometimes aggressive, territorial. Pairs bond easily.

Diet: Seed mixture for large parakeets, manufactured diets; fresh fruits and vegetables, some sprouts; calcium, mineral, and vitamin supplements.

Housing:
Degree of Difficulty: 2
Voice: ♩
Size: 10¼ in.

QUICK INFO Order: *Parrots* Family: *Parrots* (→ p. 6)
Distribution: *Argentina, Bolivia, Brazil.*

Greenfinch

Carduelis chloris

Housing: 🏠 🏭
Degree of Difficulty: 1
Voice: 🎵
Size: 6 in.

Description: Female less brightly colored than male. Several possible colors. Warbling, ringing, twittering song; good imitators. Open nester.

Housing: Indoor (40×20×20 in.) or outdoor aviary with frost-free shelter (3×3 ft.). Vegetation of evergreen trees, branches on mesh of indoor aviary. Floor sand or concrete with good drainage. Food, water, and bathing containers on floor.

Living Conditions: Birds are very robust. Freestanding nest in undergrowth; nesting aids: pockets of heather, nesting basket, commercially manufactured nest; nest materials: grasses, twigs, plant and animal wool. Four to six eggs, incubation 13 days. Reliable nesters.

Social Behaviors: Argumentative during mating season; keep mating pair isolated during this time. May be kept with other types of finches at other times.

Diet: Small seeds containing carbohydrates and primarily oils (→ p. 246), weed and grass seeds, foxtail millet, sprouted food, green food, fruits and berries, fresh branches with buds, live food; grit in limited amounts.

QUICK INFO **Order:** *Sparrows* **Family:** *Finches (→ p. 17)* **Distribution:** *Europe and northern Africa, Asia Minor to Trans-Caspian region.*

Green Twinspot

Mandingoa nitidula

Housing: 🖽 🏠 🏘
Degree of Difficulty: 3
Voice: 🎵
Size: 3½–4½ in.

Description: Female less brightly colored than the male; the red or orange hues are more olive. Song consists of warbling and pure whistling tones. Lively. Open nester.

Housing: Cage or indoor aviary (32×16×16 in.) or outdoor aviary with shelter (3×3 ft., no cooler than 68°F / 20°C). Vegetation of bushes and shrubs, but with some open areas. Floor sand with good drainage. Place food, water, and bathing containers near ground level.

Living Conditions: Twelve- to fourteen-hour day with aid of light. Nest only in aviary with abundant vegetation. Free-standing nest in undergrowth; nesting aid: nesting box; nest materials: grasses, plant fibers, moss, feathers, dirt. Four to six eggs, incubation 12–13 days.

Social Behaviors: May be kept with other Green Twinspots and other Estrildidae.

Diet: Small-grained varieties of millet, canary grass seed, soaked wheat and oats, foxtail millet, sprouted food, weed and grass seeds, green food, soft food; grit in limited amounts.

QUICK INFO Order: *Sparrows* **Family:** Estrildidae (Waxbills and allies) (→ p. 18) **Distribution:** *Sierra Leone to the Congo and northern Angola, Kenya, and Ethiopia; in eastern Africa south to southern South Africa, Bioko Island.*

Green-winged Macaw

Ara chloroptera

Housing:
Degree of Difficulty: 3
Voice:
Size: 35–37½ in.

Description: Male and female look the same. Loud, squawking voice; good mimic. Cavity nester.

Housing: All-metal indoor aviary or outdoor aviary (12×6×6 ft.; wire thickness ³⁄₁₆ in.), with shelter (6×3 ft., no cooler than 68°F / 20°C) and sprinkler installation. Floor concrete with good drainage. Natural wood perches and climbing branches; provide something to keep birds occupied (→ p. 242). Keep food, water, and bathing containers off ground.

Living Conditions: Likes to bathe. Needs 60–70% humidity; spray regularly. Cavities in natural wood trunks or nesting boxes (28×22×39 in., entry hole about 10 in.); provide approximately 4 in. wood shavings and peat moss. Two to three eggs, incubation 25–27 days.

Social Behaviors: Solitary birds with close family ties; keep mating pair by themselves.

Diet: Seed mixture for large parrots, manufactured diets (→ p. 246), half-ripe and sprouted foods, fruit, vegetables, green food, shrimp meal, live food; twigs for gnawing.

QUICK INFO **Order:** *Parrots* **Family:** *Parrots* (→ *p. 6*)
Distribution: *Paraguay and northern Argentina to Venezuela, Colombia, and eastern Panama.*

Hahn's Macaw

Diopsittaca nobilis

Housing:
Degree of Difficulty: 2
Voice: 🔊
Size: 12 in.

Description: The smallest Macaw. Male and female look the same. Loud, squawking call; good mimics. Become friendly. Cavity nester.

Housing: All metal indoor or outdoor aviary (54×72×54 in., wire thickness ¹⁄₁₆ in.) and sprinkler installation. Floor concrete. Branches for perching and climbing; provide something to keep birds occupied (→ p. 242). Keep food, water, and bathing containers elevated in shelter.

Living Conditions: Likes to bathe. Nesting cavity in thick-walled natural tree trunk (inside diameter 15 in., 24–32 in. deep, entry hole 4 in.). Two to four eggs, incubation 25 days. Successful nester.

Social Behaviors: Bird kept alone needs "family bonding." Keep mating pair by themselves.

Diet: Seed mixture for large parrots, manufactured diets (→ p. 246), half-ripe sprouted food, fruits, vegetables, green food, shrimp meal or live food; fresh twigs for gnawing.

QUICK INFO Order: *Parrots* Family: *Parrots* (→ p. 6)
Distribution: *Venezuela and Guyana to Brazil.*

Himalayan Greenfinch

Corduelis spinoides

Also: *Chloris spinoides*

Housing:	⊞ 🏠 🗃
Degree of Difficulty:	2
Voice:	♫
Size:	5–5½ in.

Description: Female same color as the male, but not as bright. Warbling, ringing song. Open-nester.

Housing: Cage or indoor aviary (32×16×16 in.) or outdoor aviary with frost-free shelter (3×3 ft.). Vegetation with evergreen trees and bushes. Floor sand; good drainage. Food, water, and bathing containers on ground.

Living Conditions: Relatively undemanding. Deep bowl-shaped nest freestanding in undergrowth; nesting aids: basket, commercially manufactured nest; nest materials: grasses, moss, roots, twigs, plant wool, animal hair. Four to six eggs, incubation 13–14 days. Successful breeding attempts.

Social Behaviors: Argumentative during breeding season; mating pair should be kept by themselves. At other times may be kept with other finches.

Diet: Small seeds containing carbohydrates and mainly oils (→ p. 246), weed and grass seeds, foxtail millet, sprouted food, green food, fruit and berries, fresh twigs with buds; grit in limited amounts.

QUICK INFO **Order:** *Sparrows* **Family:** *Finches* (→ p. 17) **Distribution:** *Himalayan region from Pakistan to western Myanmar.*

Hooded Siskin

Carduelis magellanicus

Also: *Spinus magellanicus*

Description: Female less brightly colored than the male, with less yellow. Warbling, twittering song. Lively. Open nester.

Housing: Cage or indoor aviary (32×16×16 in.) or outdoor aviary with shelter (3×3 ft., no cooler than 68°F /20°C). Vegetation consisting of bushes or evergreen trees; attach branches to cage wire. Floor sand with good drainage. Keep food, water, and bathing containers elevated.

Living Conditions: Robust, but sensitive to damp and cold. Freestanding nest in undergrowth; nesting aids: nesting basket, half-open nesting box; nest materials: plant fibers, hay, moss, roots. Three to four eggs, incubation 12–13 days.

Social Behaviors: Sometimes cantankerous during mating season; at other times may be kept with other Finches.

Diet: Seeds containing oils (→ p. 246), lettuce seeds; Niger seed is especially important; fig and pine seeds, half-ripe seeds of composite flowers, berries, fruits, green food, buds, egg and live food; grit in limited amounts.

Housing: [icons]
Degree of Difficulty: 1
Voice: [icon]
Size: 4½ –4¾ in.

QUICK INFO **Order:** *Sparrows* **Family:** *Finches* (→ *p. 17*) **Distribution:** *Southern Colombia, southern Venezuela and Guyana to southern Argentina, northern Chile, Uruguay.*

Hyacinth Macaw

Anodorhynchus hyacinthinus

Description: Male and female look the same; juveniles have shorter tails. Strong fliers; loud voice. Often forages on the ground. Very hard chewer. Nests in hollows, holes, or crevices.

Housing: Cage or indoor aviary (3×2½×6 ft.); outdoor aviary with shelter (30×9×8 ft., at least 50°F / 10°C). Concrete floor with good drainage. Provide food and water containers off the ground; branches or chunks of wood for chewing.

Living Conditions: Enjoys showering or bathing. Eager breeder. Heavy wooden nest box (24×28×40 in., entry hole 9 in.). One to two eggs; incubation 28–29 days.

Social Behaviors: Friendly, curious. Can be aggressive when breeding.

Diet: Seed mixture for large parrots, manufactured diets, fruits and vegetables, raw nuts, animal protein, vitamin and mineral supplements.

Housing:
Degree of Difficulty: 3
Voice:
Size: 40 in.

QUICK INFO **Order:** *Parrots* **Family:** *Parrots* (→ p. 6)
Distribution: *Bolivia, Brazil, Paraguay.*

Indian Silverbill

Lonchura malabarica

Also: White-throated Munia
Euodice malabarica

Housing:	
Degree of Difficulty: 1	
Voice:	
Size: 4½–4¾ in.	

Description: Male and female look the same. Song consists of short, purring, twittering stanzas. Lively. Open nester.

Housing: Cage or indoor aviary (32×16×16 in.) or outdoor aviary with shelter (3×3 ft., no cooler than 59°F / 15°C). Thick vegetation, but leave flying room. Floor sand with good drainage. Install food, water, and bathing containers near ground level.

Living Conditions: Undemanding. Twelve- to fourteen-hour day with aid of light. Mating pair should be able to select each other in flock; nesting aids: half-open or closed nesting box; nest materials: grasses, plant fibers, animal wool, feathers. Three to six eggs, incubation approximately 12 days.

Social Behaviors: Several mating pairs may be kept together and with other Estrildidae species.

Diet: Small- and large-grained varieties of millet, canary grass seed, soaked wheat and oats, foxtail millet, sprouted food, weed and grass seeds, green food; grit in limited amounts.

QUICK INFO **Order:** *Sparrows* **Family:** Estrildidae (Waxbills and allies) (→ p . 18) **Distribution:** *Sri Lanka, India to the Himalayas, west as far as Afghanistan, eastern coast of the Gulf of Oman.*

Japanese Grosbeak

Coccothraustes personatus

Also: *Eophona personata*

Description: Female same color as the male, but not as bright. Soft, whispering song. Open nester.

Housing: Indoor aviary (62×32×32 in.) or outdoor aviary with shelter (3×3 ft., no cooler than 50°F / 10°C). Lush vegetation consisting of evergreen trees and bushes. Floor sand with good drainage. Keep food, water, and bathing containers elevated.

Living Conditions: Robust bird species. Remains shy and tempestuous, so unsuited to cage living. Freestanding nest in undergrowth or hidden in evergreen boughs on wall; nesting aid: nesting box; nest materials: grasses, roots, moss, lichens, plant fibers, plant and animal wool. Three to six eggs, incubation 11–12 days. Successful breeding attempts.

Social Behaviors: Peaceable. May be kept with other Japanese Grosbeaks and other small birds.

Diet: Small seeds containing carbohydrates and especially oils (→ p. 246); foxtail millet; sprouted food; green food; fruits and berries; fresh twigs with buds; live food; grit.

Housing: 🏠 🏢
Degree of Difficulty: 2
Voice: 🎵
Size: 9 in.

QUICK INFO **Order:** *Sparrows* **Family:** *Finches* (→ *p. 17*)
Distribution: *Southeastern Siberia to Manchuria, northern Japan.*

Java Sparrow

Padda oryzivora

Housing: ⊞ 🏠 🗄
Degree of Difficulty: 1
Voice: 🎵
Size: 5½ in.

Description: Male and female look the same. Several colors possible. Melodious song with chortling, warbling, and bell sounds. Likes to fly. Open nester.

Housing: Cage or indoor aviary (48×24×36 in.) or outdoor aviary with shelter (3×3 ft., no cooler than 64°F / 18°C). Vegetation of bushes; leave space for flying. Floor sand or concrete with good drainage. Keep food, water, and bathing containers near ground level.

Living Conditions: Undemanding and robust. Twelve- to fourteen-hour day with aid of light. Likes to bathe. Mating pair should be able to select each other in flock. Nesting aids: oblong parakeet nesting box, half-open or closed nesting box; nest materials: coconut fibers, grass stalks, moss, or bast. Five to six eggs, incubation 13–14 days. Easy breeders.

Social Behaviors: May be kept in aviary with other Java Sparrows and other Estrildidae.

Diet: Small- and large-grained varieties of millet, canary grass seed, soaked wheat and oats, foxtail millet, sprouted food, weed and grass seeds, green food; grit in limited amounts.

QUICK INFO Order: *Sparrows* **Family:** *Estrildidae (Waxbills and allies)* (→ p. 18) **Distribution:** *Java and Bali, adapted to southeastern Asia, among other places.*

Jenday Conure

Aratinga jandaya

Housing: 🏠 🏠 🏠
Degree of Difficulty: 2
Voice: 🔊
Size: 12 in.

Description: Male and female look the same; juveniles less brightly colored. Shrill, loud voice. Strong, rapid flier. Hard chewer.

Housing: Indoor cage or aviary (24×24×48 in.); outdoor aviary with shelter (9×3×6 ft., nest boxes to protect from cold). Provide food and water containers off the floor; natural branches for perching and chewing.

Living Conditions: Likes to bathe. Cavity brooder. Wooden nest box (10×10×20 in., entry hole 2½ in.). Three to five eggs; incubation 23 days.

Social Behaviors: Friendly, curious. Can be kept with other *Aratinga* species even during breeding season.

Diet: Seed mixture for large parakeets; manufactured diets; fresh fruits and vegetables; wild greens; sprouts; mineral, vitamin, and calcium supplements.

QUICK INFO **Order:** *Parrots* **Family:** *Parrots* (→ p. 6)
Distribution: *Brazil*.

Laughing Dove

Streptopelia senegalensis

Description: Female less brightly colored than male. Laughing, chortling voice. Open nester.

Housing: Indoor or outdoor aviary (9×3×6 ft.) with shelter (6×3 ft., no cooler than 68°F / 20°C). Vegetation consisting of bushes or small trees. Floor dirt, bowl with sand for sand baths. Keep food, water, and bathing containers on ground.

Living Conditions: Easy keeper. Adaptable. Flat nest in undergrowth; nesting aids: board, flat basket, bowl or small, open wooden box slightly elevated; nest materials: small twigs, blades of grass, shredded paper. Separate independent young birds from older birds. Two eggs, incubation 13 days. Reliable nester.

Social Behaviors: Aggressive toward other Laughing Doves and other dove species during mating season. May be kept with other bird species.

Diet: Mixture of seeds containing carbohydrates and oils (→ p. 246), weed and grass seeds, foxtail millet, sprouted food; grit or sand.

Housing: 🏠 🏠
Degree of Difficulty: 1
Voice: 🎵
Size: 10¼–11 in.

QUICK INFO Order: *Doves* Family: *Doves* (→ *p. 6*)
Distribution: *India, Near East, Africa south of the twentieth parallel.*

Lavender Waxbill

Estrilda caerulescens

Also: *Glaucestrilda caerulescens*

Description: Male and female look the same. Twittering song, various calls. Curious. Likes to fly and climb. Open nester.

Housing: 🔲 🏠
Degree of Difficulty: 2
Voice: 🎵
Size: 4¼–4½ in.

Housing: Cage or indoor aviary (32×16×16 in.). Vegetation of bushes and grass. Floor sand with good drainage. Place food, water, and bathing containers near ground level.

Living Conditions: Keep no cooler than 68°F / 20°C. Twelve- to fourteen-hour day with aid of light. Provide daily exercise periods outside of cage for cage-kept birds. Freestanding nest in undergrowth; also moves into nests of other birds; nesting aids: nesting box or nesting basket; nest materials: long grasses, plant fibers, flock, small feathers. Three to five eggs, incubation 13–15 days.

Social Behaviors: During mating season aggressive toward other Lavender Waxbills and closely related species, and may chase them to exhaustion; peaceable toward other Estrildidae.

Diet: Small-grained varieties of millet, canary grass seed, foxtail millet, half-ripe or sprouted weed and grass seeds, green food; grit in limited amounts.

QUICK INFO **Order:** *Sparrows* **Family:** *Estrildidae (Waxbills and allies)* (→ p. 18) **Distribution:** *Senegal through Cameroon as far as Chad.*

Lemon-breasted Seedeater

Serinus citrinipectus

Also: *Ochrospiza citrinipectus*

Description: Female the same color as the male, but without yellow breast. Warbling, twittering song. Lively. Open nester.

Housing: Indoor aviary (32×16×16 in.) or outdoor aviary with shelter (3×3 ft., no cooler than 50°F / 10°C). Vegetation, including grasses and bushes; leave an open area. Floor sand with good drainage. Place food, water, and bathing containers close to ground.

Living Conditions: Nest in undergrowth; nesting aids: nesting basket, commercially manufactured nest, nesting block; nest materials: dried grasses, plant fibers, sisal and coconut fibers, flax, feathers, flock, moss. Three to four eggs, incubation approximately 13–14 days. Reliable brooders.

Social Behaviors: Incompatible with other Lemon-breasted Seedeaters. May be kept with other small birds.

Diet: Seeds containing oils and carbohydrates (→ p. 246), foxtail millet, sprout food, green food, apples, berries, a little live food; grit in limited quantities.

Housing:
Degree of Difficulty: 1
Voice:
Size: 4¼–4¾ in.

QUICK INFO **Order:** *Sparrows* **Family:** *Finches* (→ *p. 17*)
Distribution: *Southern Zambia, Malawi, Mozambique, northern South Africa.*

Lesser Sulfur-crested Cockatoo

Cacatua sulphurea

Also: *Small Sulfur-crested Cockatoo*
Description: Male with dark iris; female's is reddish brown. Loud squawk. Cavity nester.

Housing: 🏠 🏢
Degree of Difficulty: 2
Voice: 🔊
Size: approximately 13 in.

Housing: All-steel indoor or outdoor aviary (6×3×3 ft.) with shelter (3×3 ft., no cooler than 60°F / 15°C). Concrete floor with 6-in. cover of sand-dirt mixture. Branches for perching and climbing; provide something to keep birds occupied (→ p. 242). Leave room to fly. Keep food, water, and bathing containers elevated.

Living Conditions: Spray. Change floor covering yearly. Check for worms. Nesting cavity in natural tree trunk or nesting box (12–14×12–14×24–32 in., entry hole 4–4¾ in.). Two to three eggs, incubation approximately 27 days.

Social Behaviors: Keep mating pair by themselves during mating season. Single birds can be kept with other parrots of the same size.

Diet: Seed mixture for cockatoos, manufactured diets (→ p. 246), sprouted food, fruit, vegetables, green food; softwood branches for gnawing.

QUICK INFO **Order:** *Parrots* **Family:** *Cockatoos* (→ p. 6) **Distribution:** *Lesser Sunda Islands, Sulawesi and offshore islands.*

Lineolated Parakeet

Bolborhynchus lineola

Description: Female the same color as the male, but with less black on tail. Soft, twittering voice. Good climber. Cavity nester.

Housing: Indoor or protected outdoor aviary (36×18×18 in., wire thickness ¾₄ in.) and sprinkler. Perching and climbing branches at least 1½ in. thick. Keep food, water, and bathing containers elevated.

Living Conditions: Provide shade. Likes to bathe in the rain. Check claws. Nesting cavity in natural tree trunk or nesting box (10×10×12 in., entry hole 2½ in.); put in some wood shavings or moist peat moss. Four to five eggs, incubation 18–20 days.

Social Behaviors: May be kept with other Lineolated Parakeets, peaceable parakeets, and birds of other species.

Diet: Various types of millet, canary grass seed, oats, Niger seed, weed and grass seeds, foxtail millet, sprouted food, plenty of fruits, vegetables, and green food, egg food; softwood branches for gnawing; offer manufactured diet.

Housing: 🏠 🏤
Degree of Difficulty: 2
Voice: 🎵
Size: 6¼–6¾ in.

QUICK INFO **Order:** *Parrots* **Family:** *Parrots* (→ p. 6) **Distribution:** *Southern Mexico to central Peru, Bolivia, and northwestern Venezuela.*

Long-tailed Rosefinch

Uragus sibiricus

Housing:
Degree of Difficulty: 1
Voice: ♩
Size: 5¾–6¾ in.

Description: Female same color as the male, but all red areas are brownish beige. Soft, monotone song, persistent singer. Can become friendly. Lively. Open nester.

Housing: Indoor (48×20×20 in.) or outdoor aviary with shelter (3×3 ft., no cooler than 50°F / 10°C). Vegetation of bushes and shrubs. Floor sand; good drainage. Keep food, water, and bathing containers elevated.

Living Conditions: Undemanding. Robust. Freestanding nest on a tree trunk in vegetation; nesting aids: commercial nest, nesting basket; nest materials: sticks, fine roots, coconut fibers. Three to five eggs, incubation 13–14 days.

Social Behaviors: Incompatible with other Long-tailed Rosefinches and similarly colored birds during mating season. At other times may be kept with small birds.

Diet: Small seeds containing carbohydrates and mainly oils (→ p. 246), weed and grass seeds, foxtail millet, sprouted food, green food, fruits and berries, fresh twigs with buds, live food; grit in limited amounts.

QUICK INFO **Order:** *Sparrows* **Family:** *Finches (→ p. 17)*
Distribution: *Western Siberia to Ussuri Region, Mongolia, northwestern and Central China, northern Japan.*

Madagascar Red Foudy

Foudia madagascariensis

Housing:
Degree of Difficulty: 2
Voice:
Size: 5–5½ in.

Description: Male in display plumage red and brown; in dull plumage, colored gray-brown like the female. High, chirping song like cricket, deep and melodic. Lively and fond of exercise. Open nester.

Housing: Indoor aviary (40×16×16 in.) or outdoor aviary with covered corner and shelter (3×3 ft., no cooler than 50°F / 10°C). Vegetation consisting of low bushes. Leave flying room free. Floor sand. Place food, water, and bathing containers near ground level.

Living Conditions: Very fond of bathing. Keep one male with several females. Roofed nest low in vegetation; nest materials: sisal and hemp fibers, grasses. Three to four eggs, incubation 12–14 days. Breeding attempts frequently successful.

Social Behaviors: Aggressive toward other Madagascar Red Foudies and similarly colored birds during mating season. Peaceable at other times.

Diet: Various weed seeds; millet; oats and canary grass seed, whether sprouted, ripe, or half ripe; fruits; lots of green food; live and egg food; grit in limited amounts.

QUICK INFO **Order:** *Sparrows* **Family:** *Weavers* *(→ p. 20)*
Distribution: *Madagascar and other places, adapted to Seychelles, Comoro Islands, and St. Helena.*

Magpie Mannikin

Lonchura fringilloides

Also: *Spermestes fringilloides*

Description: Female the same color as the male, but smaller. Song a series of whistling tones. Open nester.

Housing: Cage or indoor aviary (48×20×20 in.) or outdoor aviary with shelter (3×3 ft., no cooler than 59°F / 15°C). Vegetation consisting of bushes. Floor sand with good drainage. Keep food, water, and bathing containers slightly elevated.

Living Conditions: Undemanding and robust. Very fond of bathing. Twelve- to fourteen-hour days with aid of light. When several birds are kept together, they all sleep together in the same nest. Freestanding nest in shrubbery; nesting aids: nesting basket, commercially manufactured nest; nest materials: grasses, coconut and sisal fibers. Four to six eggs, incubation 13–14 days.

Social Behaviors: May be kept as several mating pairs and with other Estrildidae.

Diet: Small- and large-grained varieties of millet, canary grass seed, soaked wheat and oats, foxtail millet, sprouted food, weed and grass seeds, green food; grit in limited amounts.

Housing:
Degree of Difficulty: 1
Voice: ♪
Size: 4¾–5¼ in.

QUICK INFO Order: *Sparrows* **Family:** *Estrildidae (Waxbills and allies) (→ p. 18)* **Distribution:** *Gambia as far as Sudan and east coast to Kenya, south as far as South Africa, Angola.*

131

Mannikin Finch

Lonchura striata var. domestica

Description: Male and female look the same. Several colors possible. Voice a chattering twitter. Open nester.

Housing: Cage or indoor aviary (32×16×16 in.). Floor sand with good drainage. Perches of natural wood. Keep food, water, and bathing containers elevated.

Living Conditions: Easy keepers. Undemanding. Albinos have a tendency to eye disease. Keep in pairs during breeding season, otherwise multiple females will disturb one another while brooding. Provide ready-made nest of plant fibers and hay in basket or half-open box; they have no nest-building instinct. Five to six eggs, incubation 18–19 days.

Social Behaviors: Peaceable. May be kept with other Estrildidae or seed eaters.

Diet: Small- and large-grained varieties of millet, a bit of canary grass seed, Niger seed, hulled oats, foxtail millet, sprouted food, weed and grass seeds, green food, live food; grit in limited amounts.

Housing:
Degree of Difficulty: 1
Voice: ♩
Size: 4½–5½ in.

QUICK INFO **Order:** *Sparrows* **Family:** *Estrildidae (Waxbills and allies)* (→ p. 18) **Distribution:** *Original form lives in southern and southeastern Asia.*

Maroon-bellied Conure

Pyrrhura frontalis

Housing: ⊞ 🏠 🏫
Degree of Difficulty: 2
Voice: ♩
Size: 10¼ in.

Description: Male and female look the same. Social, friendly. Quiet voice. Fast fliers. Not hard chewers.

Housing: Cage or indoor aviary (18×18×24 in.); outdoor aviary (9×3×6 ft., nest boxes to protect from cold). Provide food, water, and bathing containers off the ground; branches for climbing and chewing.

Living Conditions: Enjoys showers or bathing in containers. Sometimes sleeps in nest box. Prolific breeder. Wooden nest box (10×10×10 in.). Three to nine eggs, incubation 23–25 days.

Social Behaviors: Bold, sometimes aggressive, territorial. Pairs bond easily.

Diet: Seed mixture for large parakeets; manufactured diets; fresh fruits and vegetables; sprouts; calcium, mineral, and vitamin supplements.

QUICK INFO Order: *Parrots* **Family:** *Parrots* (→ p. 6)
Distribution: *Argentina, Bolivia, Brazil, Paraguay, Uruguay.*

Masked Grassfinch

Poephila personata

Description: Male and female look the same. Song a sonorous, warbling twitter. Likes exercise. Open nester.

Housing: Indoor aviary (48×20×20 in.) or outdoor aviary with shelter (3×3 ft., no cooler than 68°F / 20°C). Vegetation consisting of bushes; leave open flying room. Floor sand with good drainage. Food, water, and bathing containers near ground level.

Living Conditions: Sensitive to damp cold. Twelve- to fourteen-hour day with the aid of a light. Likes to bathe. Must be able to fly, otherwise tends to gain weight. Mating pair should be able to select each other in flock. Cylindrical nest in vegetation; nesting aid: half-open nesting box in hidden area. Nest materials: plant fibers, grasses, moss, flock. Four to six eggs, incubation 13–14 days.

Social Behaviors: May be kept with several mating pairs and other Estrildidae species.

Diet: Small- and large-grained varieties of millet, canary grass seed, soaked wheat and oats, foxtail millet, sprouted food, weed and grass seeds, green food; grit in limited amounts.

Housing:
Degree of Difficulty: 2
Voice:
Size: 4½ in.

QUICK INFO **Order:** *Sparrows* **Family:** *Estrildidae (Waxbills and allies)* (→ p. 18) **Distribution:** *Northwestern Australia, south to the nineteenth parallel.*

Masked Lovebird

Agapornis personata

Housing:
Degree of Difficulty: 1
Voice: 🎵 📢
Size: 6–6¼ in.

Description: Male and female look the same. Numerous colors possible. Loud twittering and chatting. Nimble flier. Cavity nester.

Housing: Cage or indoor aviary 36×18×18 in.), outdoor aviary (wire thickness ¾₄ in.) with frost-free shelter (36×18 in.). Floor sand. Branches for perching and climbing; opportunities to keep occupied (→ p. 242). Food, water, and bathing containers on ground.

Living Conditions: Robust. Daily exercise outside of cage for cage-kept birds. Likes to bathe. Mating pair should be able to select each other in flock. Nesting cavity in nesting box or tree trunk (10×6×8 in., entry hole 2 in.) put in moist peat moss; nest materials: pieces of bark, twigs. Four to five eggs, incubation 22–23 days.

Social Behaviors: Keep flock in large aviary and mating pair by themselves in cage, since they are quite argumentative.

Diet: Seed mixture for parakeets, manufactured diets; (→ p. 246), foxtail millet, sprouted food, fruits, vegetables, green food; cuttlebone; twigs for gnawing.

QUICK INFO **Order:** *Parrots* **Family:** *Parrots* (→ p. 6) **Distribution:** *Eastern and southern Tanzania.*

Maximilian's Pionus

Pionus maximilani

Also: Scaly-headed Parrot

Description: Male and female look the same. Cavity brooders. Moderately noisy; not hard chewers. Swift, agile fliers.

Housing: Cage or indoor aviary (22×28×15 in.); outdoor aviary (8½×3×6 ft., at least 50°F / 10°C) with bare floor and good drainage. Provide food and water containers off the ground; perches, swings.

Living Conditions: Sometimes prefers showers to bathing. Breeds regularly. Wooden nest box (12×12×24 in., entry hole 4 in.) with pine shavings. Three to four eggs, incubation 26 days.

Social Behaviors: Sometimes shy or moody; easily stressed in new situations. Does well with other Pionus species.

Diet: Seed mixture for large parrots, manufactured diets, fruits and vegetables, nuts, sprouts, nutritional supplements.

Housing:
Degree of Difficulty: 2
Voice:
Size: 11½ in.

QUICK INFO Order: *Parrots* **Family:** *Parrots* (→ p. 6)
Distribution: *Argentina, Bolivia, Brazil, Venezuela.*

Mealy Amazon

Amazona farinosa

Housing:
Degree of Difficulty: 2
Voice:
Size: 15–17 in.

Description: Male and female look the same. Shrieks loudly; good imitator. Cavity nester.

Housing: All-metal indoor or outdoor aviary (9×3×6 ft., metal thickness ⁵⁄₆₄ in.) with shelter (6×3 ft., no cooler than 50°F / 10°C) and sprinkler. Floor concrete. Branches for perching and climbing; opportunities to keep occupied (→ p. 242). Keep food, water, and bathing containers elevated.

Living Conditions: Provide twelve-hour days yearlong with daylight lamp. Spray two to three times a week. Nesting hole in natural tree trunk (inside diameter 12 in., depth 24–32 in., entry hole 4–5 in.); provide climbing aids for female and young birds inside. Three eggs, incubation 25–27 days.

Social Behaviors: May be kept with other parrot species, even smaller ones.

Diet: Seed mixture for Amazons, manufactured diets (→ p. 246), sprouted food, half-ripe seeds, green food, fruits and vegetables, twigs with buds for gnawing.

QUICK INFO Order: *Parrots* Family: *Parrots* (→ p. 6)
Distribution: *From southern Mexico through Mesoamerica to Bolivia and southern Brazil.*

Melba Finch

Pytilia melba

Housing: 🏠
Degree of Difficulty: 2
Voice: 🎵
Size: 4½–5 in.

Description: Female same color as male, but without red face mask. Gurgling, whistling song. Open nester.

Housing: Indoor aviary (48×20×20 in.). Thick vegetation in one corner. Floor sand or concrete with good drainage. Place food, water, and bathing containers close to ground level.

Living Conditions: Melba Finches are hardy. Twelve- to fourteen-hour day with aid of a light. Freestanding nest in vegetation; nesting aids: half-open nesting box, commercially manufactured nesting box; nest materials: grasses, coconut fibers, lots of feathers. Four to six eggs, incubation 12–13 days. Easy breeders, but poor success if the birds don't get enough live food.

Social Behaviors: Male aggressive with other birds and other redheaded finches. May be kept with smaller finches without red head.

Diet: Various types of small millet seeds, canary grass seed and foxtail millet, weed and grass seeds, green food, small live food or egg food; grit in limited amounts.

QUICK INFO **Order:** *Sparrows* **Family:** *Finches (→ p. 17)* **Distribution:** *Tropical Africa south of the Sahara.*

Meyer's Parrot

Poicephalus meyeri

Housing:	
Degree of Difficulty: 2	
Voice:	♩
Size: 9 in.	

Description: Male and female look the same. Voice fairly quiet, good imitators. Can become friendly. Fast fliers. Sleeps in cavities. Cavity nester.

Housing: All-metal indoor or outdoor aviary (36×18×18 in., wire thickness ⁵⁄₆₄ in.) with shelter (18×36 in., no cooler than 50°F / 10°C). Floor sand, preferably concrete; good drainage. Branches for climbing and perching; opportunities to keep occupied (→ p. 242). Keep food, water, and bathing containers elevated.

Living Conditions: Robust birds. Provide spray baths. Nesting cavity in natural tree trunk or nesting box (8–10×8–10×24 in., entry hole 2¼–2¾ in.); provide interior climbing aid for female and young birds. Two to four eggs, incubation 27 days.

Social Behaviors: Keep breeding pair by themselves during mating season. May be kept with birds from other families.

Diet: Seed mixture for large parrots, manufactured diets (→ p. 246), foxtail millet, sprouted food, half-ripe corn, weed and grass seeds, fruits, vegetables; twigs for gnawing.

QUICK INFO Order: *Parrots* Family: *Parrots* (→ p. 6) Distribution: *Central and eastern Africa.*

139

Mitred Conure

Aratinga mitrata

Housing: 🏠
Degree of Difficulty: 2
Voice: 🔊
Size: 15 in.

Description: Female the same color as the male, but with smaller red mask. Harsh, loud voice; good mimic. Good flier. Very lively, curious, playful. Can become friendly. Cavity nester.

Housing: All-metal outdoor aviary (3×6×3 ft., wire thickness ⁵⁄₆₄ in.) with shelter (6×3 ft., no cooler than 50°F / 10°C). Floor concrete. Branches for perching and climbing; opportunities to keep occupied (→ p. 242). Place food, water, and bathing containers near ground level.

Living Conditions: A robust bird species. Likes to bathe. Nesting hole in natural tree trunk or nesting box (12×12×20–24 in., entry hole 2¾ in.). They gnaw nesting hole, so provide cavity with extra-thick floor. Two to five eggs, incubation 25–26 days.

Social Behaviors: Aggressive toward other Mitred Conures and related species, even in neighboring aviary. May be kept with Estrildidae, doves, or chickens.

Diet: Seed mixture for large parakeets, manufactured diets (→ p. 246), foxtail millet, sprouted food, corncobs, green food, fruits and berries; branches for gnawing.

QUICK INFO **Order:** *Parrots* **Family:** *Parrots* (→ p. 6)
Distribution: *Central Peru, Bolivia to northwestern Argentina.*

Moluccan Cockatoo

Cacatua moluccensis

Also: Salmon-crested Cockatoo

Description: Male and female look the same; sometimes females have smaller heads; reddish irises. Loud voice; strong flier; hard chewer.

Housing: 🏠🏠🏠
Degree of Difficulty: 2
Voice: 🔊
Size: 20¾ in.

Housing: Cage or indoor aviary (36×36×48 in.); outdoor aviary with shelter (24×9×6 ft. at least 41°F / 5°C). Wooden perches; regular supply of wood for chewing; provide food, water, and bathing containers off the ground.

Living Conditions: Likes showers, bathing. Cavity brooder; sometimes reluctant to breed. Nest box (22×18×15 in.); two to three eggs, incubation 30 days.

Social Behaviors: Male frequently aggressive to mate during breeding season. Avoid colony situations; often aggressive to other species.

Diet: Seed mixture for cockatoos, manufactured diets, nuts, greens, vegetables, some fruits, vitamin and mineral supplements.

QUICK INFO **Order:** *Parrots* **Family:** *Parrots* (→ p. 6)
Distribution: *Australia, Indonesia, New Zealand.*

Mulga Parakeet

Psephotus varius

Housing:
Degree of Difficulty: 2
Voice: 🎵
Size: 10½ in.

Description: Male colorful, female brownish olive with red wing patch. Soft warbling, chattering voice. Cavity nester.

Housing: Indoor or outdoor aviary (6×3×3 ft., wire thickness ⁵⁄₆₄ in.) with shelter (3×3 ft., no cooler than 59°F / 15°C). Plenty of vegetation, but don't restrict flying room. Branches for perching and climbing. Floor dirt and grass for digging. Place food, water, and bathing containers near ground level.

Living Conditions: Sensitive to damp and cold. Check regularly for worms. Cavity in natural tree trunk or nesting box (8–10×8–10×16–20 in., entry hole 2¼–3 in.); put in 1¼ in. of decayed wood. Four to six eggs, incubation 19–20 days.

Social Behaviors: Keep mating pair by themselves; incompatible with other Mulga Parakeets and closely related species, even in adjacent aviary.

Diet: Seed mixture for large parakeets, manufactured diets (→ p. 246), foxtail millet, sprouted food, weed and grass seeds, fruits, green food; charcoal; twigs for gnawing.

QUICK INFO Order: *Parrots* Family: *Parrots* (→ p. 6)
Distribution: *Australia south of the tropic from the west coast to the southeast.*

Nanday Conure

Nandayus nenday

Also: Black-hooded Parakeet

Description: Male and female look the same. Loud, screeching voice. Strong fliers. Sometimes forages on the ground. Hard chewers.

Housing: Cage or indoor aviary (24×24×48 in.); outdoor aviary with shelter (9×3×6 ft., nest boxes to protect from cold); concrete floor; nest boxes for roosting. Provide food and water containers off the floor; natural branches for perching and chewing.

Living Conditions: Enthusiastic bathers. Cavity nesters. Wooden nest box (10×10×16 in., entry hole 2½ in.). Four to five eggs; incubation 24–25 days.

Social Behaviors: Playful, active; accepts other birds of similar size.

Diet: Seed mixture for large parakeets; manufactured diets; fresh fruits and vegetables; wild greens; nuts; sprouts; mineral, vitamin, and calcium supplements.

Housing:
Degree of Difficulty: 2
Voice:
Size: 12 in.

QUICK INFO Order: *Parrots* Family: *Parrots* (→ p. 6)
Distribution: *Argentina, Bolivia, Brazil, Paraguay.*

143

Orange Bishop

Euplectes franciscanus

Description: Male in mating plumage red and black; in plain plumage, brown like the female. In confinement the red pales to orange. Hissing, croaking song. Open nester.

Housing: 🏢 🏠 🏫
Degree of Difficulty: 2
Voice: ♩
Size: 5 in.

Housing: Cage or indoor aviary (48×20×20 in.) or outdoor aviary with shelter (3×3 ft., no cooler than 50°F / 10°C). Vegetation of bushes and reeds. Perches. Floor sand. Place food, water, and bathing containers on floor.

Living Conditions: Like to bathe. At breeding time, keep one male with three to four females. Freestanding nest in vegetation; nesting aids: commercially manufactured nesting box, half-open nesting box; nest materials: grasses, panicum, leaves. Three to four eggs, incubation 14 days.

Social Behaviors: During breeding season incompatible with males of the same species. May be kept with other seed eaters.

Diet: Seeds containing carbohydrates and (a little) oil (→ p. 246), weed and grass seeds, foxtail millet, sprouted food, green and soft foods; grit in limited amounts. Fruits and sun are important for maintenance of red plumage.

QUICK INFO **Order:** *Sparrows* **Family:** *Weavers* (→ p. 20)
Distribution: *Senegal, Cameroon to Ethiopia, Somalia, south to northern Uganda and central Kenya.*

Orange-cheeked Waxbill

Estrilda melpoda

Description: Male and female look the same. Lively, likes to fly. Open nester.

Housing: Cage or indoor aviary (32×16×16 in.) or protected outdoor aviary with shelter (3×3 ft., no cooler than 64°F / 18°C). Vegetation consisting of bushes and small evergreen trees, leave open areas. Floor sand with good drainage. Place food, water, and bathing containers near ground level.

Living Conditions: Undemanding and robust. Twelve- to fourteen-hour day with aid of light. Likes to bathe. Free-standing covered nest in undergrowth or (rarely) in half-open nesting box (6×6×6 in.), parakeet box or nesting basket; nest materials: plant fibers, grasses. Four to six eggs, incubation 12 days. Sensitive to disturbance, so successful nesting is difficult.

Social Behaviors: May be kept with several mating pairs and other calm Estrildidae Finch species.

Diet: Small- and large-grained varieties of millet, canary grass seed, Niger seed, foxtail millet, sprouted foods, weed and grass seeds, green food; grit in limited amounts.

Housing:
Degree of Difficulty: 1
Voice: ♩
Size: 4 in.

QUICK INFO **Order:** *Sparrows* **Family:** *Estrildidae (Waxbills and allies)* (→ p. 18) **Distribution:** *Senegal and Liberia as far as Chad and northern Angola.*

Orange-chinned Parakeet

Brotogeris j. jugularis

Description: Male and female look the same, juveniles darker. Moderately noisy. Swift fliers. Cavity nesters. Hard chewers.

Housing: Cage or indoor aviary (48×16×20 in.); outdoor aviary in summer (7½×3×6 ft., at least 50°F / 10°C). Branches or rotten wood for chewing; provide food and water containers off the ground.

Living Conditions: Not avid bathers. Rotted tree stumps for nesting, or wooden boxes (7×7×14 in.). Two to nine eggs; incubation 23 days.

Social Behaviors: Aggressive if kept with other parakeets in aviaries or cages that are too small; compatible with some finches.

Diet: Seed mixture for parakeets, manufactured diets, fresh fruits and vegetables, vitamins.

Housing: ⊞ 🏠
Degree of Difficulty: 2
Voice: ♩
Size: 7 in.

QUICK INFO Order: *Parrots* **Family:** *Parrots* (→ p. 6)
Distribution: *Mexico, Colombia, Venezuela.*

146

Orange-headed Ground Thrush

Zoothera citrina

Also: *Geokichla citrina*

Description: Female colored like the male, but not as bright. Warbling, twittering song. Become friendly, but remain easily startled. Open nester.

Housing: Indoor aviary (32×16×24 in.) or outdoor aviary with a shelter (3×3 ft., no cooler than 68°F / 20°C). Fairly thick vegetation with evergreen trees and bushes; also provide vegetation outside along one side; put a few stones, some roots, and a fairly thick branch on the ground; keep part of the ground clear. Floor sand with good drainage. Place food, water, and bathing containers close to ground level.

Living Conditions: Fairly robust. Clean floor covering every day or two. Freestanding nest in vegetation; nesting aids: nesting basket, nesting block; nest materials: dried grasses, twigs, moss. Four eggs, incubation 14 days.

Social Behaviors: Peaceable. May be kept with other Orange-headed Ground Thrushes and other small birds.

Diet: Soft food for thrushes, egg food, live food; fewer berries than other thrushes.

Housing:
Degree of Difficulty: 2
Voice:
Size: 8½ in.

QUICK INFO Order: *Sparrows* **Family:** *Thrushes (→ p. 13)* **Distribution:** *Southern India to southern China, Indochina, Southeast Asia, a few southeast Asia Islands.*

147

Orange-winged Amazon

Amazona Amazonica

Description: Male and female look the same. Loud squawk, also whistle. Can become friendly. Lively. Cavity nester.

Housing: All-metal indoor or outdoor aviary (6×3×3 ft., wire thickness ⁵⁄₄ in.) with shelter (3×3 ft., no cooler than 50°F / 10°C). Sprinkler. Floor concrete. Branches for perching and climbing; opportunities to keep occupied (→ p. 242). Keep food, water, and bathing containers elevated.

Living Conditions: Likes to bathe. Spray two to three times per week; needs high humidity. Cavity in nesting box (12×12×24–32 in., entry hole 4–5 in.). Resents nest checks. Three to four eggs, incubation 25–27 days.

Social Behaviors: Keep mating pair by themselves during breeding season; at other times may be kept with other Orange-winged Amazons and other Amazons.

Diet: Seed mixture for Amazons, manufactured diets (→ p. 246), foxtail millet, sprouted food, half-ripe weed and grass seeds, green food, fruits and vegetables; twigs with buds for gnawing.

Housing: 🏠 🏢
Degree of Difficulty: 2
Voice: 🔊
Size: 12¼–13 in.

QUICK INFO Order: *Parrots* Family: *Parrots* (→ p. 6)
Distribution: *Northern Venezuela to southern Brazil, Trinidad and Tobago.*

Oriental Magpie Robin

Copsychus saularis

Housing: 🖼️ 🏠 🏢
Degree of Difficulty: 1
Voice: 🎵
Size: 8 in.

Description: Male black and white, female dark gray and white. Rising whistling, trilling, chattering song. Open nester.

Housing: Indoor aviary (32×16×16 in.) or outdoor aviary with shelter (3×3 ft., no cooler than 68°F / 20°C). Thick vegetation; provide a few stones, roots, and a fairly thick branch on the ground, plus open floor space. Floor sand or concrete with good drainage. Place food, water, and bathing containers near ground level.

Living Conditions: Undemanding. Likes to bathe. Freestanding nest in vegetation; nest aids: half-open or closed nesting box (8×8×12 in.); nest materials: plant fibers, moss, animal hair. Three to six eggs, incubation 12–13 days. Successful breeding attempts.

Social Behaviors: Intolerant of other birds during breeding season. May be kept in an aviary with other seed eaters. May also be kept alone in a cage.

Diet: Coarse soft food for thrushes, green food, vegetables, berries, fruit; grit or cuttlebone.

QUICK INFO **Order:** *Sparrows* **Family:** *Thrushes (→ p. 13)*
Distribution: *Western Pakistan to southern China, from Malaysia and Greater Sunda Islands to the Philippines.*

Oriental White-eye

Zosterops palpebrosus

Housing: 🏠 🏢
Degree of Difficulty: 2
Voice: 🎵
Size: 4–4½ in.

Description: Female similar to male, but less brightly colored. Soft, ringing song. Lively. Friendly. Open nester.

Housing: Indoor aviary (60×32×48 in.), or outdoor aviary protected from wind and rain, with shelter (3×3 ft., no cooler than 68°F / 20°C). Thick vegetation. Floor lined with birdcage litter. Keep food, water, and bathing containers elevated.

Living Conditions: Change or clean floor covering and furnishings every day or two. Likes to bathe in a bowl or damp leaves. Provide twelve-hour day all year long. Freestanding nest in vegetation; nesting aids: nesting basket, half-open nesting box; nest materials: plant fibers, cotton, plant and animal wool. Two to four eggs, incubation 10–11 days.

Social Behaviors: Incompatible with other Oriental White-eyes and related species. May be kept with other small birds such as Estrildidae Finches.

Diet: Nectar drink for White-eyes, soft fruit, fine soft food, live food; food containing carotene to keep colors from fading.

QUICK INFO Order: *Sparrows* **Family:** *White-eyes*
(→ *p. 15*) **Distribution:** *India and Pakistan to southwestern China and Vietnam, Malaysia, Greater Sunda Islands.*

Pacific Parrotlet

Forpus coelestis

Also: Celestial Parrotlet

Description: Female has no blue; green eye streak. Different colors possible. Chirping, chattering voice. Cavity breeders.

Housing: Cage or indoor aviary (18×18 in.; 48×16×20 in. preferable). Natural wood perches. Provide food, water, and bathing containers off the ground.

Living Conditions: Swings for perching and sleeping. Bathing preferences vary. Budgerigar-sized or grandfather-style nest boxes (10×10×7 in., entry hole 2 in.), with pine shavings. Six to eight eggs, incubation 21 days.

Social Behaviors: Territorial; aggressive to other birds and animals. Not suitable for mixed aviaries.

Diet: Seed mixture for parakeets; fresh fruits and vegetables; greens; sprouts; whole-grain breads; vitamin, mineral, and calcium supplements; offer manufactured diets.

Housing:

Degree of Difficulty: 2

Voice: ♩

Size: 5¼ in.

QUICK INFO Order: *Parrots* Family: *Parrots* (→ p. 6)
Distribution: *Ecuador, Mexico, Peru.*

Painted Finch

Emblema picta

Description: Female similar to male, but less red. Quiet song. Becomes friendly. Open nester.

Housing: Indoor (32×16×16 in.) or outdoor aviary with shelter (3×3 ft., no cooler than 68°F / 20°C). Vegetation: thick bushes, open ground surface. Floor clean sand, roots, or rock chips with good drainage. Attach boards to wall about three ft. off the ground for sleeping. Place food, water, and bathing containers close to ground level.

Living Conditions: Twelve- to fourteen-hour day with aid of lamp. Sensitive to dampness and cold. Sunbathing should be possible. Clean floor covering every day or two, and replace yearly. Ball-shaped nest in undergrowth; nesting aids: half-open nesting box, nesting basket; nest materials: twigs, coconut fibers, grass, plant wool, feathers, bark, charcoal. Three to five eggs, incubation 16–18 days.

Social Behaviors: Peaceable. Several mating pairs can be kept together and with other finches.

Diet: Small and large-grained varieties of millet, reed canary grass seed, foxtail millet, sprouted food, weed and grass seeds, green food; grit in limited quantities.

Housing: 🏠 🏢
Degree of Difficulty: 2
Voice: ♩
Size: 4 in.

QUICK INFO **Order:** *Sparrows* **Family:** *Estrildidae (Waxbills and allies)* (→ p. 18) **Distribution:** *Northern and central Australia.*

Parson's Finch

Poephila cincta

Housing:			
Degree of Difficulty: 1			
Voice: ♫			
Size: 4½ in.			

Description: Female the same color as the male, but not as bright. Slightly smaller throat patch. Gabbling, warbling song. Likes to fly. Cavity nester.

Housing: Cage or indoor aviary (32×16×16 in.) or outdoor aviary with shelter (3×3 ft., no cooler than 59°F / 15°C). Floor sand; good drainage. Place food, water, and bathing containers near ground level.

Living Conditions: Twelve- to fourteen-hour day with aid of light. Likes to bathe. Mating pair should be able to select each other in flock. Freestanding nest in vegetation; nesting aids: half-open or closed nesting box, commercially manufactured nest; nest materials: grasses, plant wool, plant fibers, moss, feathers. Five to nine eggs, incubation 12 days.

Social Behaviors: Aggressive toward other Parson's Finches and related species. May be kept with larger Estrildidae or birds of other species.

Diet: Small-grained varieties of millet, canary grass seed, Niger seed, foxtail millet, sprouted food, weed and grass seeds, green food, live food; grit in limited quantities.

QUICK INFO **Order:** *Sparrows* **Family:** *Estrildidae (Waxbills and allies)* (→p. 18) **Distribution:** *Northern and northeastern Australia.*

153

Peach-faced Lovebird

Agapornis roseicollis

Housing: 🪟 🏠 🏚
Degree of Difficulty: 1
Voice: 🔊
Size: 6–7 in.

Description: Male and female look the same. Different colors possible. Loud voice. Good flier. Cavity nester.

Housing: Cage or indoor aviary (36×18×18 in., wire thickness ¹⁄₁₆ in.) with frost-free shelter (18×36 in.), floor sand. Branches for perching and climbing; opportunities to keep occupied (→ p. 242). Food, water, and bathing containers near ground level.

Living Conditions: Daily exercise session on climbing tree for cage dwellers. Likes to bathe. Mating pair should be able to select each other in flock. Nesting hole in nesting box (10×6×8 in., entry hole 2 in.); provide damp peat moss; nest material: pieces of bark, twigs. Three to six eggs, incubation 23 days.

Social Behaviors: A flock may be kept in a large aviary; keep mating pair by themselves in cage.

Diet: Seed mixture for parakeets (→ p. 246), foxtail millet, sprouted food, fruits, vegetables, green food, and cuttlebone; twigs for chewing apart; offer manufactured diet.

QUICK INFO Order: *Parrots* Family: *Parrots* (→ p. 6) Distribution: *Southwestern Angola as far as the north of Cape Province.*

Pekin Robin

Leiothrix lutea

Also: *Chinese Nightingale*

Description: Female the same color as the male, but not as bright. Melodious, warbling song. Lively. Can become friendly. Open nester.

Housing: Degree of Difficulty: 1 — Voice: 🎵 — Size: 6 in.

Housing: Cage or indoor aviary (32×16×24 in.) or outdoor aviary with frost-free shelter (3×3 ft.). Thick vegetation consisting of bushes. Floor sand. Place food, water, and bathing containers near ground level.

Living Conditions: Robust species. A few hours of daily free flight for cage-kept birds. Like to sun themselves. Freestanding nest in undergrowth; nesting aids: board, basket, horizontal twigs; nest materials: coconut and sisal fibers, grasses, fine roots, raffia, dry leaves. Three to four eggs, incubation 13 days.

Social Behaviors: Incompatible with other Pekin Robins and closely related species. A mating pair may be kept with other species.

Diet: Soft foods containing insects, lots of small live food, nectar drink, fruits and berries, green foods, various types of millet and canary grass seed; grit in a small bowl.

QUICK INFO **Order:** *Sparrows* **Family:** *Babblers* (→ p. 14)
Distribution: *Southern China through Myanmar to Pakistan.*

Peter's Twinspot

Hypargos niveoguttatus

Housing: 🏠 🏢
Degree of Difficulty: 2
Voice: 🎵
Size: 5–5¼ in.

Description: Female the same color as the male, but without red on head. Trilling, warbling song; even females sing. Open nester.

Housing: Indoor aviary (48×20×20 in.) or outdoor aviary with shelter (3×3 ft., no cooler than 68°F / 20°C). Thick vegetation, provide branches for perching (birds sleep on a high branch). Floor sand with good drainage. Hide live food inside. Place food, water, and bathing containers near ground level.

Living Conditions: Fourteen-hour day with help of light. Free-standing nest on ground or in undergrowth; nesting aids: nesting basket, half-open nesting box high among branches; nesting materials: grass, coconut fibers, feathers, flock. Separate independent young birds from older birds. Three to five eggs, incubation 12–13 days.

Social Behaviors: Aggressive toward other Peter's Twinspots and red-colored birds. Peaceable with other Estrildidae.

Diet: Small- and large-grained varieties of millet, canary grass seed, sprouted food, weed and grass seeds, green food, fruits and blooms, live food; grit in limited amounts; charcoal.

QUICK INFO **Order:** *Sparrows* **Family:** *Estrildidae (Waxbills and allies)* (→ p. 18) **Distribution:** *Mozambique, Zimbabwe, Zambia, Zaire, and Tanzania.*

Pictorella Finch

Lonchura pectoralis

Housing: 🏠 📊
Degree of Difficulty: 1
Voice: ♩
Size: 4¾ in.

Also: *Heteromunia pectoralis*

Description: Female the same color as the male, but head brownish black. Chirps like a sparrow. Can become friendly. Open nester.

Housing: Indoor aviary (32×16×16 in.) or roofed outdoor aviary with shelter (3×3 ft., no cooler than 64°F / 18°C). Provide warm areas. Thick vegetation consisting of shrubs, grass, and clumps of reeds; open areas with large roots or stones. Floor sand; good drainage. Food, water, and bathing containers near ground level.

Living Conditions: Twelve- to fourteen-hour day with aid of light. Check claws regularly. Mating pair should be able to select each other in flock. Nest in vegetation or on ground; nesting aids: half-open nesting box, nesting basket; nest materials: soft and hard grasses, plant fibers, twigs, fine roots, pine needles. Three to five eggs, incubation 14 days.

Social Behaviors: May be kept with other Pictorella Finches and other finch species.

Diet: Mixture of millet, canary grass seed, and grass seeds—ripe, half-ripe, and sprouted; foxtail millet; live food; grit in limited amounts.

QUICK INFO **Order:** *Sparrows* **Family:** *Estrildidae (Waxbills and allies)* (→ p. 18) **Distribution:** *Northern Australia.*

Pin-tailed Parrot Finch

Erythrura prasina

Description: Female less brightly colored than the male, scarcely any blue on head and throat, no red on belly. Rattling, crackling, chirping song. Lively, good flier; very timid. Open nester.

Housing: Indoor aviary (60×20×20 in.) or protected outdoor aviary with shelter (3×3 ft., no cooler than 68°F / 20°C, or no cooler than 77°F / 25°C during mating season). Vegetation consisting of bamboo, reeds, evergreen trees; leave sufficient flying room. Floor sand or concrete; adequate drainage. Keep food, water, and bathing containers elevated.

Living Conditions: Likes to bathe. Twelve- to fourteen-hour days with aid of light. Check claws regularly. Freestanding nest in undergrowth; nesting aids: half-open or closed nesting box; nest materials: small leaves, plant fibers, moss. Two to six eggs, incubation 12–14 days.

Social Behaviors: Occasionally cantankerous with other Pin-tailed Parrot Finches. May be kept with other Estrildidae.

Diet: Small- and large- grained varieties of millet, canary grass seed, soaked wheat and oats, sprouted food, weed and grass seeds, green food, fruits; grit in limited amounts.

Housing: 🏠 🏤
Degree of Difficulty: 3
Voice: 🎵
Size: 5½–6 in.

QUICK INFO **Order:** *Sparrows* **Family:** *Estrildidae (Waxbills and allies)* (→ p. 18) **Distribution:** *Laos, Thailand, Malaysia, Sumatra, Borneo, Java.*

Pintail Whydah

Vidua macroura

Housing: 🏠 🏠
Degree of Difficulty: 2
Voice: ♩
Size: 5–13 in.

Description: Male in display plumage black and white with long middle tail feathers; female and male in plain plumage are same sparrow color. Typical song shrill, twittering, rasping; also sings like host bird. Parasitizes broods of Common Waxbill (→ p. 81) and Black-rumped Waxbill (→ p. 47).

Housing: Indoor aviary (48×20×20 in.) or outdoor aviary with shelter (3×3 ft., no cooler than 59°F / 15°C). Thick vegetation, lots of open flying room. Floor surface sand. Provide branches for perching and singing. Place food, water, and bathing containers on and above ground level.

Living Conditions: Likes to bathe. For successful breeding, birds must be kept with several mating pairs of host birds. One egg per host bird nest.

Social Behaviors: Can be kept with host birds and other seed eaters in large aviary.

Diet: Seeds containing carbohydrates and (a little) oil (→ p. 246), weed and grass seeds, foxtail millet, sprout food, green food, fruit, vegetables; grit in limited amounts.

QUICK INFO **Order:** *Sparrows* **Family:** *Weavers* (→ p. 20)
Distribution: *Nearly all of Africa south of the Sahara.*

Plum-headed Parakeet

Psittacula cyanocephala

Housing:	🏠 🏡
Degree of Difficulty: 1	
Voice:	🎵 🔊
Size:	13–14½ in.

Description: Female the same color as the male, but head blue-gray without red wing spot. Several colors possible. Soft, melodic voice, shrill flight call. Quickly becomes friendly. Good climber and flier. Cavity nester.

Housing: Indoor or outdoor aviary (6×3×3 ft., wire thickness ⁵⁄₆₄ in.) with shelter (3×3 ft., no cooler than 50°F / 10°C). Floor sand or concrete. Branches for perching and climbing; opportunities to keep busy (→ p. 242). Keep food, water, and bathing containers elevated.

Living Conditions: Sensitive to dampness and cold. Nesting cavity in nesting box (10×10×16–20 in., entry hole 2½ in.); put in decayed wood. Sensitive to disturbance during mating season. Four to six eggs, incubation 22–23 days. Breeding attempts frequently successful.

Social Behaviors: May be kept with other Plum-headed Parakeets and birds of other species.

Diet: Various types of millet, canary grass seed, unhusked oats and wheat, seeds containing only a little oil (→ p. 246), fruits, sprouted food, egg food; twigs for gnawing; offer manufactured diets.

QUICK INFO Order: *Parrots* Family: *Parrots* (→ p. 6)
Distribution: *Sri Lanka, Indian subcontinent.*

Princess of Wales Parakeet

Polytelis alexandrae

Also: Alexandra Parakeet

Housing: 🏠 🏡
Degree of Difficulty: 2
Voice: 🔊
Size: 16½–18 in.

Description: Female less brightly colored than the male, with shorter tail. Several possible colors. Loud, warbling, cackling voice. Likes to fly, but is also found on the ground. Cavity nester.

Housing: Indoor or outdoor aviary (9×3×6 ft., wire ⁵⁄₆₄ in.) with shelter (3×6 ft., at least 50°F / 10°C) and sprinkler system. Sand floor. Natural branches for sitting and climbing, clear floor. Provide containers for food, drinking water, and bathing on floor.

Living Conditions: Likes to bathe. Check regularly for worms. Nesting cavity in natural tree trunk or nesting box (10–11×10–11 in.×24 in., entry hole 3 in.); provide decayed wood, bevel holes. Four to six eggs; incubation 20–21 days.

Social Behaviors: Peaceable. May be kept with other parakeets as well as birds from other groups.

Diet: Seed mixture for large parakeets (→ p. 246), manufactured diets, foxtail millet, immature grass and weed seeds, sprout food, green food, fruit and berries.

QUICK INFO Order: *Parrots* Family: *Parrots* (→ p. 6) Distribution: *Australian outback*.

Purple Glossy Starling

Lamprotornis purpureus

Description: Male and female look the same. Whistling, chattering call. Curious, lively. Good flier. Cavity nester.

Housing: Indoor aviary (48×24×36 in.) or outdoor aviary with shelter (6×3 ft., no cooler than 68°F / 20°C). Vegetation consisting of evergreen and flowering bushes. Absorbent floor covering (birdcage litter). Place food, water, and bathing containers on ground.

Living Conditions: Robust species. Likes to bathe. Clean or change floor covering and furnishings every day or two. Nest in large nesting box (12×12×16 in., entry hole usually high up, 2½–2¾ in.); lots of nest materials: twigs, leaves, plant fibers, grasses. Separate independent young birds from older birds. Two to three eggs, incubation approximately 14 days.

Social Behaviors: May be kept with other Purple Glossy Starlings and fairly large bird species in a large aviary, but not with smaller species.

Diet: Fruits and berries, green food, coarse soft food containing insects, hamburger, live food.

Housing:
Degree of Difficulty: 2
Voice:
Size: 9–10 in.

QUICK INFO **Order:** *Sparrows* **Family:** *Starlings* (→ p. 21)
Distribution: *Senegal, Cameroon, Uganda, western Kenya.*

Purple Grenadier

Uraeginthus ianthinogaster

Also: *Granatina ianthinogaster*

Description: Male chestnut brown and shiny blue, female cinnamon brown. Sonorous song with warbling and cracking noises. Open nester.

Housing: Indoor (40×20×20 in.) or outdoor aviary with shelter (3×3 ft., 72–77°F / 22–25°C during the day, no cooler than 68°F / 20°C at night). Thick vegetation. Floor sand with good drainage. Place food, water, and bathing containers on ground.

Living Conditions: Need warmth. Provide opportunities for sunbathing. Twelve- to fourteen-hour day with aid of light. Freestanding nest in vegetation; nesting aids: basket, commercially manufactured nest, or half-cavity nesting box; nest materials: plant fibers, coconut and sisal fibers, dried grass. Three to five eggs, incubation 13–14 days.

Social Behaviors: Aggressive toward other Purple Grenadiers and closely related species; peaceable with other Estrildidae.

Diet: Small-grained varieties of millet; canary grass seed; foxtail millet; ripe, half-ripe, and sprouted weed and grass seeds; green food; grit in limited amounts.

Housing:
Degree of Difficulty: 2
Voice:
Size: 5½ in.

QUICK INFO **Order:** *Sparrows* **Family:** *Estrildidae* (→ p. 18) **Distribution:** *Somalia across Kenya and eastern Uganda to Tanzania.*

Purple Honeycreeper

Cyanerpes caeruleus

Description: In display plumage, male blue-purple and black; in plain plumage, greenish like female. Thin, peeping scratchy song. Lively movements through underbrush. Open nester.

Housing: 🏠 🏤
Degree of Difficulty: 2
Voice: ♪
Size: 4½ in.

Housing: Indoor aviary (32×16×16 in.) or outdoor aviary with shelter (3×3 ft., no cooler than 64–68°F / 18–20°C). Thick vegetation with blossoming bushes, bamboo, and bulb plants. Absorbent floor covering (birdcage litter, beech wood chips). Branches for perching. Elevated food, water, and bathing containers.

Living Conditions: Clean or change floor covering and furnishings every day or two. Likes to bathe. Bowl-shaped nest freestanding in undergrowth. Nesting aids: small box or basket camouflaged in branches; nesting materials: grass stalks, coconut fibers, and roots. Two eggs, incubation 12–14 days.

Social Behaviors: Incompatible with other Purple Honeycreepers and related species. May be kept with other small birds in the aviary.

Diet: Fruits, berries, vegetables, soft food, live food, nectar.

QUICK INFO Order: *Sparrows* Family: *Buntings* (→ p. 15) Distribution: *Panama to Bolivia, Trinidad, Tobago.*

Purple-naped Lory

Loris domicella

Also: Black-capped Lory

Description: Male and female look alike. Raspy voice; good imitators. Quickly becomes friendly. Curious. Likes to climb and fly. Sleeps in cavities. Cavity nester.

Housing: 🏢
Degree of Difficulty: 2
Voice: 🔊
Size: 11 in.

Housing: All-metal outdoor aviary (6 × 3 × 3 ft., wire thickness ¹⁄₁₆ in.) with shingled shelter (3 × 3 ft., 10 cooler than 50°F / 10°C) and sprinkler. Vegetation including bushes with blossoms. Floor 6 in. / 15 cm coarse gravel or concrete; good drainage. Natural branches for perching and climbing; provide something to keep bird occupied (→ p. 242). Keep food, water, and bathing containers off floor.

Living Conditions: Clean furnishings and floor daily. Nesting cavity in a natural tree trunk or a nesting box (10 × 10 × 50 in., entry hole 4 in.). Two eggs, incubation 23–24 days.

Social Behaviors: Keep mating pair by themselves; very aggressive.

Diet: Lorikeet mix (→ p. 249), pollen, soft fruit, seeds containing carbohydrates (→ p. 246), sprouted food, live food, fresh branches with buds and blossoms.

QUICK INFO **Order:** *Parrots* **Family:** *Parrots (→ p. 6)* **Distribution:** *Seram and Ambon islands (South Moluccas).*

Quaker (Monk) Parakeet

Myiopsitta monachus

Description: Male and female look the same. Various colors possible. Voice is a loud shriek. Becomes friendly. Only species of parrot that doesn't nest in cavities. Open nester.

Housing:
Degree of Difficulty: 1
Voice:
Size: 11½–12 in.

Housing: All-metal outdoor aviary (6 × 3 × 3 ft., wire thickness ⁵⁄₆₄–⁷⁄₆₄ in.) with frost-free shelter (3 × 3 ft.). Floor concrete. Provide branches for climbing and perching. Keep food, water, and bathing containers elevated.

Living Conditions: Provide large base made of sticks, or strong wire nest topped by a nest made of twigs 20 in. long; also accepts nesting box (6 × 10 × 16 in., entry hole 3 in.) with a nest of twigs inside. Five to eight eggs, incubation 26 days.

Social Behaviors: May be kept with other Quaker (Monk) Parakeets and other parrots only in a very large aviary.

Diet: Seed mixture for large parakeets; manufactured diets (→ p. 246), foxtail millet, corncobs (both also half ripe), cooked corn, green food, carrots, fruits and berries; fresh branches for gnawing.

QUICK INFO Order: *Parrots* Family: *Parrots* (→ p. 6)
Distribution: *Southern Bolivia, Paraguay, Uruguay, southern Brazil, northern Argentina.*

Rainbow Lorikeet

Trichoglossus haematodus

Housing:
Degree of Difficulty: 2
Voice:
Size: 10–12 in.

Description: Male and female look the same. Loud and squawking to soft and prattling. Lively, fond of climbing. Cavity nester.

Housing: All metal outdoor aviary (6 × 3 × 3 ft.) with shelter (3 × 3 ft., no cooler than 50°F / 10°C) and sprinkler. Shrubbery. Floor 6 in. of coarse gravel. Natural wood branches for climbing and perching; provide something to keep bird occupied (→ p. 242). Keep food, water, and bathing containers elevated.

Living Conditions: Clean furnishings and floor covering daily. Nesting holes in natural wood tree trunks or nesting boxes (8 × 8 × 24 in., entry hole 3–4 in.); provide 4–6 in. of decayed wood or wood shavings. Two to three eggs, incubation 25 days.

Social Behaviors: May be kept together with friendly species that do not build nests in cavities.

Diet: Lorikeet mix (→ p. 249), pollen, fruit, starchy seeds, sprouted food, live food, twigs with buds.

QUICK INFO Order: *Parrots* Family: *Parrots* (→ p. 6)
Distribution: *From Bali to New Guinea, Bismarck Archipelago and Solomon Islands as far as New Caledonia and the New Hebrides, plus North, East, and South Australia.*

Red-billed Firefinch

Lagonosticta senegala

Housing:
Degree of Difficulty: 1
Voice: 🎵
Size: 3½–4 in.

Description: Male red and brown, female mainly yellow and gray to olive green. Melodious song. Open nester.

Housing: Indoor aviary (32×16×16 in.) or outdoor aviary with shelter (3×3 ft., no cooler than 64°F / 18°C). Vegetation consisting of low bushes; leave fairly large open area for searching for food. Floor sand with good drainage. Place food, water, and bathing containers on ground.

Living Conditions: Undemanding. Sensitive to damp cold. Twelve- to fourteen-hour day with aid of light. Freestanding nest in undergrowth or in pine branches; nesting aids: half-open nesting box, nesting basket; nest materials: soft grasses, raffia, sisal and coconut fibers, fine wool threads and feathers. Three to four eggs, incubation 11–12 days. Reliable nesters.

Social Behaviors: May be kept with other Red-billed Firefinches and other Estrildidae.

Diet: Small- and large-grained varieties of millet, canary grass seed, foxtail millet, sprouted food, weed and grass seeds, green food, fine soft food, live food; small amounts of grit.

QUICK INFO **Order:** *Sparrows* **Family:** *Estrildidae (Waxbills and allies)* (→ p. 18) **Distribution:** *Senegal to Ethiopia, south to South Africa.*

Red-cheeked Cordon Bleu

Uraeginthus bengalus

Housing:
Degree of Difficulty: 1
Voice: ♩
Size: 4³⁄₄ in.

Description: Female colored like the male, but without red ear patch. Hoarse, pinched song; females also sing. Lively. Open nester.

Housing: Cage or indoor aviary (32×16×16 in.) or sheltered outdoor aviary with shelter (3×3 ft., no cooler than 68°F / 20°C). Emergency lighting inside shelter. Vegetation consisting of thorny shrubbery and evergreen trees. Floor sand with adequate drainage. Place food, water, and bathing containers on ground.

Living Conditions: Twelve- to fourteen-hour day with help of light. Freestanding nest in vegetation; nesting aids: half-open nesting box, nesting basket; nest materials: plant fibers, grasses, feathers, plant wool. Resents nest checks. Four to five eggs, incubation 11–12 days.

Social Behaviors: Aggressive toward other Red-cheeked Cordon Bleus and other closely related species during mating season; peaceable toward other species.

Diet: Small-grained varieties of millet, canary grass seed, Niger seed, foxtail millet, sprouted food, ripe and half-ripe weed and grass seeds, green food; grit in limited amounts.

QUICK INFO **Order:** *Sparrows* **Family:** *Estrildidae (Waxbills and allies) (→ p. 18)* **Distribution:** *Senegal to Ethiopia, south to Tanzania, Central Africa.*

Red-eared Parrot Finch

Erythrura coloria

Also: *Amblynura coloria*

Housing: 🏠 🏡
Degree of Difficulty: 2
Voice: 🎵
Size: 4 in.

Description: Female colored similarly to male, but not quite as bright. High, warbling song. Can become very friendly. Loves exercise. Open nester.

Housing: Indoor aviary (32×16×16 in.) or outdoor aviary with shelter (3×3 ft., no cooler than 68°F / 20°C). Thick vegetation, but with lots of flying room. Provide direct sunlight or a daylight lamp. Floor sand, or concrete with good drainage. Place food, water, and bathing containers on ground.

Living Conditions: Twelve- to fourteen-hour day with aid of a light. Likes bathing. Cylindrical nest in nesting box; nest materials: coconut fibers and blades of grass. Remove nesting box as soon as the young are three weeks old, for trouble-free raising of the first brood. Separate independent young from older birds. Two to three eggs, incubation 13–15 days. Reliable breeders.

Social Behaviors: Peaceable. May be kept with other Red-eared Parrot Finches and other finches.

Diet: Small- and large-grained varieties of millet, canary grass seeds, soaked wheat and oats, foxtail millet, sprout food, weed and grass seeds, green food; grit in limited amounts.

QUICK INFO Order: *Sparrows* Family: *Finches* (→ p. 17) Distribution: *Mindanao, Philippines.*

Red-fronted Canary

Description: Male dark brown with red forehead spot, female lighter in color. Buzzing, twittering song. Open nester.

Housing: ▦ ▣ ▥
Degree of Difficulty: 3
Voice: ♫
Size: $4\frac{1}{2}$–$5\frac{1}{4}$ in.

Housing: Cage or indoor aviary (32×16×16 in.) or outdoor aviary with shelter (3×3 ft., no cooler than 50°F / 10°C). Vegetation consisting of bushes and evergreen trees. Floor sand with good drainage. Place food, water, and bathing containers near ground level.

Living Conditions: Sometimes sensitive; then the birds need lots of light (sun or UV light) and oxygen (ionizer). Free-standing nest in undergrowth; nesting aid: nesting basket; nest materials: plant fibers, lichens, moss. Three to five eggs, incubation 13–14 days. Successful mating attempts.

Social Behaviors: Keep breeding pair by themselves during mating season. At other times may be kept with other seed eaters.

Diet: Seeds containing oils and carbohydrates (→ p. 246), ripe and nonseasonal half-ripe weed and grass seeds, foxtail millet, lots of sprouted food, green food, fruits and berries, live food, fresh twigs with buds; grit in limited quantities.

QUICK INFO **Order:** *Sparrows* **Family:** *Finches* (→*p. 17*)
Distribution: *Asia Minor, Iran, Afghanistan to Kashmir.*

Red-fronted Kakariki

Cyanoramphus novaezelandiae

Also: *Red-fronted Parakeet*

Description: Male and female look the same; juveniles have less red. Sometimes feeds on the ground; often seen near bodies of water. Soft voice. Strong fliers.

Housing: Cage or indoor aviary (18×18×24 in.); outdoor aviary (10×3×6 ft., protect from cold); concrete floor. Provide food and water containers on ground. Active, requires room to fly.

Living Conditions: Check often for worms. Enjoys bathing. Cavity nester; breeds readily. Nest box (8×8×14 in.). Four to nine eggs; incubation 20 days.

Social Behaviors: Aggressive during breeding season. Mischievous, playful, independent.

Diet: Seed mixture for large parakeets, fresh fruits and vegetables, sprouts, vitamin C and mineral supplements; offer manufactured diets.

Housing: ▨ ▣ ▨
Degree of Difficulty: 2
Voice: ♩
Size: 11 in.

QUICK INFO Order: *Parrots* **Family:** *Parrots* (→ p. 6)
Distribution: *New Zealand, outlying islands.*

Red-headed Finch

Amadina erythrocephala

Housing: 🏢 🏠 🏞
Degree of Difficulty: 1
Voice: 🎵
Size: 5–5½ in.

Description: Female less brightly colored than the male, with no red on head. Quiet, purring, twittering song. Partial cavity nester.

Housing: Cage or indoor aviary (48×20×20 in.) or outdoor aviary with shelter (3×3 ft., no cooler than 65°F / 18°C). Vegetation consisting of bushes. Floor sand with good drainage. Place food, water, and bathing containers near ground level.

Living Conditions: Robust. Undemanding. Twelve- to fourteen-hour day with aid of light. Nest in half-cavity, half-open nesting box (rarely builds own nest, moves into nests of other species); nest materials: grasses, panicum, small roots. Resents nest checks. Four to six eggs, incubation 14–15 days. Frequently nests successfully.

Social Behaviors: Keep mating pair by themselves during mating season; will take over nests of other inhabitants. At other times may be kept with other Estrildidae.

Diet: Small- and large-grained varieties of millet, canary grass seed, soaked wheat and oats, foxtail millet, sprouted food, weed and grass seeds, green food, fruits; grit in limited amounts.

QUICK INFO Order: *Sparrows* **Family:** *Estrildidae (Waybills and allies) (→ p. 18)* **Distribution:** *Angola, south as far as South Africa, central Africa.*

173

Red-headed Parrot Finch

Erythrura Psittacea

Also: *Amblynura psittacea*

Housing: Degree of Difficulty: 2
Voice:
Size: 4¾ in.

Description: Female similar to male, lighter mask, smaller. Trilling, chirping song. Lively. Likes to fly; often on ground. Nest sleeper. Open nester.

Housing: Cage or indoor aviary (32×16×16 in.) or outdoor aviary with shelter (3×3 ft., no cooler than 64°F / 18°C). Thick vegetation, or attach twigs to mesh, leave open areas. Floor sand with good drainage. Place food, water, and bathing containers near ground level.

Living Conditions: Sensitive to draft and dampness. Twelve- to fourteen-hour day with aid of light. Tends to gain weight with inadequate exercise. When removing droppings, check for worms. Likes to bathe. Freestanding nest in undergrowth; nesting aids: half-open or closed nesting box; nest materials: lots of dry grass stems, coconut fibers. Four to six eggs, incubation 13–14 days.

Social Behaviors: Peaceable. May be kept with other Red-headed Parrot Finches and other Estrildidae.

Diet: Small- and large-grained varieties of millet, canary grass seed, soaked wheat and oats, sprouted food, weed and grass seeds, green food, fruits; grit in limited quantities.

QUICK INFO Order: *Sparrows* Family: *Estrildidae (Waxbills and allies)* (→ p. 18) Distribution: *New Caledonia.*

Red-headed Quelea

Quelea erythrops

Housing:
Degree of Difficulty: 2
Voice: ♫
Size: 5 in.

Description: Male with red, female with brown head. Squeaking, hissing song. Lively. Open nester.

Housing: Indoor aviary (48×20×20 in.) or partially covered outdoor aviary protected from the wind, with shelter (3×3 ft., no cooler than 50–59°F / 10–15°C). Abundant vegetation consisting of reeds, sedge, or bamboo. Floor sand. Place food, water, and bathing containers near ground level.

Living Conditions: Robust species. Likes to bathe. Check claws regularly. Artistic hanging nest with side entrance and roof, in undergrowth; nest materials: long, fresh grasses. Two to three eggs, incubation 13 days. Repeated successful breeding attempts, so it's best to keep one male with several females.

Social Behaviors: Peaceable. May be kept with other Red-headed Queleas as well as with other fairly small birds species, such as Estrildidae.

Diet: Various types of millet and canary grass seed, dried or sprouted; weed and grass seeds; green food; not much live food; grit and cuttlebone.

QUICK INFO **Order:** *Sparrows* **Family:** *Weavers* (→ p. 20)
Distribution: *Senegal to southern Ethiopia, south to Mozambique and Angola.*

Red Lory

Eos bornea

Housing:
Degree of Difficulty: 2
Voice:
Size: 10½–12½ in.

Description: Male and female look the same. Shrill, squawking voice; good mimic. Likes to climb. Cavity nester.

Housing: All-metal outdoor aviary (6×3×3 ft., wire thickness ⅟₁₆ in.) with shelter (3×3 ft., no cooler than 50°F / 10°C) and sprinkler. Vegetation of blooming bushes. Floor 6 in. of coarse gravel. Natural wood branches for perching and climbing; opportunities to keep occupied (→ p. 242). Keep food, water, and bathing containers elevated.

Living Conditions: Robust. Clean furnishings and floor daily. Cavity in natural tree trunk or nesting box (8×8×24 in., entry hole 4 in.); put in 4–6 in. of decayed wood or wood shavings. Two eggs, incubation 24–26 days.

Social Behaviors: Keep mating pair by themselves. Only individual birds may be kept with other Lori species.

Diet: Lorikeet mix (→ p.249), pollen, soft fruits, millet, canary grass seed or sunflower seeds, sprouted food, live food, fresh twigs with buds and blossoms.

QUICK INFO Order: *Parrots* **Family:** *Parrots* (→ p. 6)
Distribution: *South Moluccas and neighboring islands.*

Red-rumped Parakeet

Psephotus haematonotus

Housing: 🏠 🏠 🏠
Degree of Difficulty: 2
Voice: 🎵
Size: 11½–12 in.

Description: Male brightly colored, female unremarkable gray-green. Melodious mating call. Frequently on ground. Cavity nester.

Housing: Cage or indoor aviary (6×3×6 ft.) or outdoor aviary (wire thickness ¾₄ in.) with shelter (3×3 ft., no cooler than 59°F / 15°C). Ample vegetation, but leave open flying room. Branches for perching and climbing. Floor dirt and grass. Place food, water, and bathing containers near ground level.

Living Conditions: Free flight for cage-kept birds. Likes to bathe. Change two to three times a week under perches. Check regularly for worms. Nesting hole in nesting box (10×10×16–20 in., entry hole 2½–3¼ in.). Four to seven eggs, incubation 19 days.

Social Behaviors: Cantankerous toward other Red-rumped Parakeets and closely related species, even in adjacent aviary, during mating season. Peaceable at other times.

Diet: Seed mixture for large parakeets, manufactured diets (→ p. 246), foxtail millet, sprouted food, weed and grass seeds, egg food, fruits and berries, green food; charcoal; fresh twigs for gnawing.

QUICK INFO Order: *Parrots* Family: *Parrots* (→ p. 6) Distribution: *Southeastern Australia except for Tasmania.*

177

Red Siskin

Carduelis cucullatus

Also: Black-headed Red Siskin, *Spinus cucullatus*

Description: Female grayer than the male, nearly without red. Red does not fade. Warbling, twittering song. Lively. Open nester.

Housing: Cage or indoor aviary (32×16×16 in.) or outdoor aviary with shelter (3×3 ft., no cooler than 68°F / 20°C). Vegetation with bushes or small trees; provide elevated branches for perching and sleeping. Floor sand with good drainage. Keep food, water, and bathing containers elevated.

Living Conditions: Likes to bathe. Freestanding nest in undergrowth; nesting aids: nesting basket, half-open nesting box; nest materials: plant fibers, plant wool, moss. Three to four eggs, incubation approximately 14 days.

Social Behaviors: Aggressive toward other Red Siskins and similarly colored birds during mating season. Peaceable at other times.

Diet: Small seeds containing oil (→ p. 246), weed and tree seeds, canary grass seeds, preferably half ripe; green food; berries and fruits; live food; grit in limited quantities.

Housing: 🐦 🐦 🐦
Degree of Difficulty: 2
Voice: 🎵
Size: 4–4½ in.

QUICK INFO Order: *Sparrows* **Family:** *Finches* (→ p. 17) **Distribution:** *Eastern Colombia, northern Venezuela, Trinidad.*

Red-whiskered Bulbul

Pycnonotus jocosus

Housing: 🏠 🏠
Degree of Difficulty: 1
Voice: 🎵
Size: 8 in.

Description: Male and female look alike. Soft, warbling, chattering song. Flies swiftly as an arrow. Lively. Open nester.

Housing: Indoor aviary (48×24×36 in.) or outdoor aviary protected from draft, with frost-free shelter (6×3 ft.). Thick vegetation with low shrubs, deciduous and evergreen trees. Absorbent floor covering because of runny droppings (bird-cage litter or beech wood chips). Keep food, water, and bathing containers elevated.

Living Conditions: Robust bird species. Undemanding. Likes to bathe. Bowl-shaped nest freestanding in undergrowth; nesting aids: half-open nesting box, nesting basket; nest materials: plant fibers, raffia, grasses, leaves. Two to three eggs, incubation 12–14 days.

Social Behaviors: Cantankerous toward other Red-whiskered Bulbuls and other birds during mating season. At other times may be kept with other fruit and insect eaters.

Diet: Soft food containing insects, nectar drink, fruits, green food, live and egg food.

QUICK INFO **Order:** *Sparrows* **Family:** *Bulbuls* (→ p. 11)
Distribution: *India to southern China and Indochina, south to Thailand and northern Malaysia.*

Regent Parrot

Polytelis anthopeplus

Housing: 🏠 🏚️
Degree of Difficulty: 1
Voice: 🎵
Size: 16 in.

Description: Female a paler green than the male, with no red wing band. Raw, trilling, warbling voice. Cavity nester.

Housing: Indoor or outdoor aviary (6×3×3 ft., wire thickness ⁵⁄₆₄ in.) with shelter (6×3 ft., no cooler than 50°F / 10°C) and sprinkler installation. Floor surface sand beneath perching and climbing branches, concrete floor. Provide something to keep birds occupied (→ p. 242). Place food, water, and bathing containers near ground level.

Living Conditions: A robust species. Offer spray baths. Change floor covering every two days. Nesting cavities in natural tree trunk or nesting box (12×12×20–24 in., entry hole 4 in.); put in decayed wood. Four to six eggs, incubation 20–21 days.

Social Behaviors: May be kept with other parrots and birds of other species.

Diet: Seed mixture for large parakeets; manufactured diets (→ p. 246), foxtail millet, sprouted food, half-ripe weed and grass seeds, fruits and berries, green food, possibly also Lorikeet mix (→ p. 249); fresh twigs for gnawing.

QUICK INFO Order: *Parrots* Family: *Parrots* (→ p. 6)
Distribution: *Southeastern and southwestern Australia.*

Rufous-bellied Niltava

Niltava sundara

Housing: 🏠
Degree of Difficulty: 2
Voice: 🎵
Size: 6¼–7 in.

Description: Male shiny blue and reddish orange, female light brown. Melodious, warbling, babbling song; good mimic. Spends lots of time on ground. Half-cavity nester.

Housing: Indoor aviary (48×24×36 in.). Provide low bushes in buckets, but leave room for flying. Floor sand. Provide branches for perching in upper part. Keep food, water, and bathing containers elevated.

Living Conditions: Robust. Mating attempts frequently successful. Nest well hidden in underbrush; nesting aids: half-open nesting box or half cavity; nest materials: stems, branches, dried leaves, roots, moss, coconut fibers. Separate independent young birds from older birds. Three to four eggs, incubation 12–13 days.

Social Behaviors: Incompatible with other Rufous-bellied Niltavas during mating season. May be kept with other birds.

Diet: Fine soft food containing insects, live food, berries, soft fruits.

QUICK INFO Order: *Sparrows* **Family:** *Flycatchers*
(→ p. 14) **Distribution:** *Pakistan, northwestern India, Myanmar, northwestern Thailand and southern China.*

Saffron Finch

Sicalis flaveola

Housing: [icons]
Degree of Difficulty: 1
Voice: [icon]
Size: 5–5½ in.

Description: Female the same color as the male, but the green is less intense. Melodious song continually repeated. Open nester.

Housing: Cage or indoor aviary (32×16×16 in.) or outdoor aviary with shelter (3×3 ft., no cooler than 59°F / 15°C). Vegetation consisting of bushes; leave free area. Floor dirt. Place food, water, and bathing containers on ground.

Living Conditions: Easy keepers. Quite robust. Nest in undergrowth; nesting aids: half-open nesting box, parakeet nesting box, commercially manufactured nest, camouflaged among branches; nesting materials: grasses, animal wool, sisal and coconut fibers. Disturb as little as possible during mating season. Three to four eggs, incubation 13–14 days. Breeding attempts often successful.

Social Behaviors: During mating season aggressive toward other Saffron Finches and other yellow birds. At other times may be kept with other seed eaters.

Diet: Mixture of seeds containing carbohydrates and oils (→ p. 246); sprouted, half-ripe, and ripe weed seeds; leaf and flower buds; live food; grit in limited amounts.

QUICK INFO **Order:** *Sparrows* **Family:** *Buntings* (→ p. 15) **Distribution:** *Venezuela to Argentina and Uruguay; naturalized in Jamaica and Panama.*

Scarlet-chested Parrot

Neophema splendida

Housing:
Degree of Difficulty: 1
Voice: 🎵
Size: $7^3/_4$–8 in.

Description: Female less brightly colored than the male, without red breast. Various colors possible. Melodious, twittering voice. Good flier, likes to climb. Often stays on ground. Cavity nester.

Housing: Indoor or outdoor aviary (36×18×18 in.; nest size ¾ in. square) with shelter (18×36 in., no cooler than 65°F / 18°C). Partly sparse undergrowth, partly open floor with grass. Natural wood perches and climbing branches. Keep food, water, and bathing containers elevated.

Living Conditions: Offer sand- and sunbaths. Nesting cavity in natural tree trunk or nesting box (8–10×8–10×12 in., entry hole 2½ in.), provide peat moss or small-animal litter; nest materials: small stalks of grass. Four to five eggs, incubation approximately 18 days.

Social Behaviors: Aggressive toward other parrots and related species, even in neighboring aviary. May be kept with Estrildidae finches, doves, or chickens.

Diet: Seed mixture for large parakeets; offer manufactured diet (→ p. 246); foxtail millet, sprouted food, green food, fruits and vegetables; twigs for gnawing.

QUICK INFO **Order:** *Parrots* **Family:** *Parrots* (→*p. 6*)
Distribution: *Southwestern and southeastern Australia.*

Senegal Parrot

Poicephalus senegalus

Housing: 🏠 🏢
Degree of Difficulty: 1
Voice: 🔊
Size: 9½ in.

Description: Male and female look the same. Voice a shrill squawk and raw twitter. Interesting courtship display. Cavity nester.

Housing: All-metal indoor or outdoor aviary (36×18×18 in., wire thickness 5⁄64 inch / 2 mm) with shelter (3×3 ft., no cooler than 50°F / 10°C). Floor concrete with drainage. Branches for perching and climbing; opportunities to keep occupied (→ p. 242). Keep food, water, and bathing containers elevated.

Living Conditions: Likes to bathe. Mating pair should be able to find each other in flock. Nesting hole in natural tree trunk or nesting box (8–10×8–10×24 in., entry hole 2¼–2¾ in.); climbing aid inside. Three to four eggs, incubation 26–28 days.

Social Behaviors: Keep mating pair alone during breeding season; also keep no birds from a similar order in the neighboring aviary. May be kept with birds from other genera.

Diet: Seed mixture for large parrots; manufactured diets (→ p 246), foxtail millet, sprouted food, weed and grass seeds, fruits, vegetables. Branches for gnawing.

QUICK INFO **Order:** *Parrots* **Family:** *Parrots* (→ p. 6)
Distribution: *From Senegal to Chad.*

Seven-colored Tanager

Tangara fastuosa

Housing:		
Degree of Difficulty: 2		
Voice: ♩		
Size: 5½ in.		

Description: Female the same color as the male, but not as bright. Lively when kept in aviary. Open nester.

Housing: Indoor or outdoor aviary (32×16×16 in.) with shelter (3×3 ft., no cooler than 64–68°F / 18–20°C). Thick vegetation with bushes or berry-producing shrubs. Floor dirt. Keep food, water, and bathing containers elevated.

Living Conditions: Relatively easy keepers. Bathe in lukewarm water in a bowl or in wet vegetation. Bowl-shaped nest free-standing in vegetation; nesting aids: nesting basket with prepared nest of dried grasses; place plant fibers, and fine roots among vegetation. Two eggs, incubation 14–15 days. Breeding attempts occasionally successful.

Social Behaviors: Sometimes incompatible with other Seven-colored Tanagers and related species during mating season; keep mating pair by themselves during that time. May be kept with other small birds.

Diet: Fruits, berries, vegetables, soft foods, live food, nectar drink.

QUICK INFO Order: *Sparrows* **Family:** *Buntings (→ p. 15)*
Distribution: *Northeastern Brazil.*

Severe Macaw

Ara severa

Housing: 🏠 🏤
Degree of Difficulty: 2
Voice: 🔊
Size: 18 in.

Description: Male and female look the same. Voice not excessively loud, good mimic. Can become friendly. Cavity nester.

Housing: All-metal indoor or outdoor aviary (9×3×6 ft., wire thickness ¾₄ in.) with shelter (3×3 ft., no cooler than 68°F / 20°C) and shower installation. Floor sand or concrete with good drainage. Natural wood branches for perching and climbing; opportunities to keep occupied (→ p. 242). Install food, water, and bathing containers high in shelter.

Living Conditions: Sprinkle or spray. Nesting cavity in a natural tree trunk, oak cask, or strong wooden nesting box (20×20×32 in., entry hole 6 in.). Two to five eggs, incubation 26–28 days.

Social Behaviors: Single bird needs family bond; several Aras can be kept together only in very large aviary.

Diet: Seed mixture for large parrots; manufactured diets (→ p. 246); half-ripe, sprouted food; fruits; green food; shrimp meal or live food; twigs for gnawing.

QUICK INFO Order: *Parrots* Family: *Parrots* (→ p. 6) **Distribution:** *Panama, northern South America to Colombia.*

Shaft-tail Finch

Poephila acuticauda

Housing:
Degree of Difficulty: 1
Voice: ♫
Size: 6³/₄ in.

Description: Male and female look the same; the two middle steering feathers are lengthened into hair-fine spikes. Voice a squeaky warbling. Lively. Becomes friendly. Open nester.

Housing: Cage or indoor aviary (48×20×20 in.), in summer outdoor aviary with shelter (3×3 ft., no cooler than 59°F / 15°C). Thick vegetation. Floor sand with good drainage. Place food, water, and bathing containers near ground level.

Living Conditions: Undemanding. Twelve- to fourteen-hour day with aid of light. Likes to bathe. Mating pair should be able to select each other in flock. Freestanding nest in undergrowth; nesting aids: basket, half-open nesting box; nest materials: grasses, plant fibers, moss, small feathers, charcoal. Separate young birds from older ones as soon as they leave the nest. Four to six eggs, incubation 13–14 days.

Social Behaviors: Aggressive toward other Shaft-tail Finches and closely related species, peaceable with other Estrildidae species.

Diet: Small- and large-grained varieties of millet; canary grass seed; foxtail millet; ripe, half-ripe, and sprouted weed and grass seeds; green food; live food; grit in limited amounts.

QUICK INFO **Order:** *Sparrows* **Family:** *Estrildidae (Waxbills and allies)* (→ p. 18) **Distribution:** *Northwestern and northern Australia.*

Siberian Blue Robin

Luscinia cyane

Also: *Larvivora cyane*

Description: Female inconspicuous brown rather than shiny blue on upper part of body. Song consisting of a variety of warbling, trilling, and chirping. Open nester.

Housing: Indoor aviary (32×16×24 in.) or outdoor aviary with a frost-free shelter (3×3 ft.). Plenty of evergreens and bushes. Floor surface covered with moss, roots, ferns, and stones. Place food, water, and bathing containers close to ground level.

Living Conditions: Robust, hardy. Capable of putting up a good fight. Nest concealed on ground or just above it in vegetation; nesting aids: nesting basket; nest materials: coconut and sisal fibers, roots. Four to six eggs, incubation 13–14 days. Breeding attempts occasionally successful.

Social Behaviors: During breeding occasionally argumentative with other birds. May be kept with other soft food eaters such as Siberian Rubythroat and Blue-winged Minla.

Diet: Soft foods containing insects, live food, lots of berries and fruits.

Housing:
Degree of Difficulty: 2
Voice:
Size: 6 in.

QUICK INFO **Order:** *Sparrows* **Family:** *Thrushes* (→ p. 13)
Distribution: *From the Altai Republic to the Ochotsk Sea, Sakhalin, the Ussuri, Manchuria, Japan, Korea.*

Silver-eared Mesia

Leiothrix argentauris

Housing: 🏠 🏘️
Degree of Difficulty: 1
Voice: 🎵
Size: 6¾ in.

Description: Female same color as the male, but more subdued. Loud twittering, warbling song. Lively. Open nester.

Housing: Indoor or outdoor aviary (6×3×6 ft.) with shelter (3×3 ft., no cooler than 54°F / 12°C). Thick vegetation to provide adequate shade. Floor sand, good drainage. Place food, water, and bathing containers near ground level.

Living Conditions: Undemanding. In summer provide direct sun. Likes to bathe. Bowl-shaped nest in vegetation; nesting aids: nesting box; nest materials: plant fibers, grass, moss, raffia. Three to four eggs, incubation 13–14 days. Reliable nesters.

Social Behaviors: Incompatible with other Silver-eared Mesias and closely related species. One mating pair may be kept with other birds.

Diet: Soft foods containing insects, lots of live food, nectar drink, fruits and berries, green food, millet and canary grass seed; grit in small bowl; mineral supplements.

QUICK INFO **Order:** *Sparrows* **Family:** *Babblers* (→ p. 14) **Distribution:** *Himalayas, southern China across Thailand to western Sumatra.*

Siskin

Carduelis spinus

Also: *Spinus spinus*

Description: Female less brightly colored than male, gray-green tuft. Twittering, warbling song. Can become friendly. Lively. Open nester.

Housing: Cage or indoor aviary (32×16×16 in.) or outdoor aviary with frost-free shelter (3×3 ft.). Vegetation including some evergreen trees and bushes. Floor sand; clean with good drainage. Keep food, water, and bathing containers elevated.

Living Conditions: Easy keepers. Freestanding nest in vegetation; nesting aids: nesting basket, nesting block, commercially made nest; nest materials: plant fibers, grass, moss, animal and plant wool. Four to five eggs, incubation 13–14 days. Reliable breeders.

Social Behaviors: Peaceable. May be kept with other Siskins and other small birds.

Diet: Seeds containing oils and carbohydrates ($\rightarrow$ p. 246); tree, weed, and grass seeds; foxtail millet; sprouted food; green food; live food; alder and birch twigs with buds; grit in limited amounts.

Housing:
Degree of Difficulty: 1
Voice:
Size: $4\frac{1}{2}$–$4\frac{3}{4}$ in.

QUICK INFO **Order:** *Sparrows* **Family:** *Finches ($\rightarrow$ p. 17)* **Distribution:** *Ireland through Siberia as far as Sakhalin and Japan.*

Snowy-headed Robin

Cossypha niveicapilla

Housing:
Degree of Difficulty: 1
Voice: 🎵
Size: 8 in.

Description: Male and female look the same, but male is larger. Warbling, twittering song; excellent mimic; females sing also. Very lively. Half-cavity nester.

Housing: Indoor or outdoor aviary (6×3×6 ft.) with shelter (3×3 ft., no cooler than 68°F / 20°C). Thick vegetation. Floor sand with good drainage. Place food, water, and bathing containers near ground level.

Living Conditions: Easy keeper. Robust. Nest in half-cavity or half-open nesting box; nest materials: pieces of wood, twigs, moss, leaves, coconut fibers. Remove the male after the eggs are laid; he usually disturbs the female while she broods. Two to three eggs, incubation 14 days. Reliable breeder.

Social Behaviors: Incompatible with other Snowy-headed Robins and even larger birds during mating season; keep mating pair by themselves during that time. At other times may be kept with other birds.

Diet: Soft foods in large flakes, live food, minced green food, fruits, berries.

QUICK INFO **Order:** *Sparrows* **Family:** *Thrushes (→ p. 13)*
Distribution: *Senegal and Sierra Leone to Sudan, southwestern Ethiopia, western Kenya and Uganda to eastern Zaire, Northern Angola.*

Society or Bengalese Finch

Lonchura striata

Description: Male and female look the same. Rattling, purring song. Likes to climb in undergrowth. Open nester.

Housing: | | |
Degree of Difficulty: 1
Voice: ♫
Size: 4¾ in.

Housing: Cage or indoor aviary (32×16×16 in.) or outdoor aviary with shelter (3×3 ft., no cooler than 64°F / 18°C). Thick vegetation. Floor sand; good drainage. Keep food, water, and bathing containers elevated.

Living Conditions: Undemanding. Twelve- to fourteen-hour day with aid of light. Likes to bathe. Large freestanding nest in vegetation or in bundle of twigs; nesting aids: half-open nesting box, commercially manufactured nest, parakeet box; nest materials: plenty of grasses, plant fibers, roots. Four to six eggs, incubation approximately 13 days.

Social Behaviors: May be kept with other Society Finches and other Estrildidae; mating pairs may disturb one another during mating season, so keep them separate.

Diet: Small-grained varieties of millet, canary grass seed, Niger seed, foxtail millet, sprouted food, weed and grass seeds, green food; small amounts of grit.

QUICK INFO Order: *Sparrows* **Family:** *Estrildidae (Waxbills and allies)* (→ p. 18) **Distribution:** *Sri Lanka, India through Myanmar to China and Taiwan, Indochina, Thailand, Malaysia, Sumatra, Andaman Islands, and Nicobar Islands.*

Spectacled Amazon

Amazona albifrons

Housing:
Degree of Difficulty: 2
Voice:
Size: 10–11½ in.

Description: Female the same color as the male, but without red on wing. Relatively loud; good mimic. Likes to climb. Cavity nester.

Housing: All-metal indoor or outdoor aviary (6×3×3 ft., wire thickness ¾ in.) with shelter (3×3 ft., no cooler than 50°F / 10°C) and sprinkler. Floor concrete. Branches for perching and climbing; opportunities to keep occupied (→ p. 242). Food, water, and bathing containers elevated.

Living Conditions: Spray two to three times per week. Mating pair should be able to select each other in flock. Nesting cavity in natural tree trunk or nesting box (inner diameter 16 in., 24–32 in. deep, entry hole 4–4¾ in.). Two to three eggs, incubation 26 days.

Social Behaviors: Keep mating pair by themselves during mating season; at other times, may be kept with other Spectacled Amazons or other Amazons.

Diet: Seed mixture for Amazons, manufactured diets (→ p. 246), sprouted food, half-ripe seeds, green foods, fruits, vegetables; twigs with buds for gnawing.

QUICK INFO Order: *Parrots* **Family:** *Parrots* (→ p. 6)
Distribution: *Western coast of Mexico, Yucatan to northern Costa Rica.*

Spice Finch

Lonchura punctulata

Housing: 🔲 🏠 🏠
Degree of Difficulty: 1
Voice: 🎵
Size: 4–5 in.

Description: Male and female look the same. Warbling, humming song, often barely audible. Lively. Open nester.

Housing: Cage or indoor aviary (32×16×16 in.) or outdoor aviary with shelter (3×3 ft., no cooler than 64°F / 18°C). Vegetation, including reeds, bushes, and small evergreen trees. Floor sand with good drainage. Keep food, water, and bathing containers near ground level.

Living Conditions: Undemanding. Twelve- to fourteen-hour days with aid of light. Check claws. Mating pair should be able to select each other in flock. Freestanding nest in undergrowth; nesting aids: nesting basket, half-open nesting box; nest materials: grass stems, roots, stalks. Five to six eggs, incubation 18–19 days. Breed more easily in outdoor aviary than in indoor one.

Social Behaviors: May be kept with other Spice Finches and other Estrildidae.

Diet: Small- and large-grained varieties of millet, canary grass seed, soaked wheat and oats, foxtail millet, sprouted food, weed and grass seeds, green food; grit in limited amounts.

QUICK INFO Order: *Sparrows* **Family:** *Estrildidae (Waxbills and allies)* (→ p. 18) **Distribution:** *India to southern China, through Malaysia, Sumatra to Celebes and to the Philippines.*

Star Finch

Neochmia ruficauda

Housing: 🏠 🏦
Degree of Difficulty: 1
Voice: 🎵
Size: 4–5 in.

Description: Female the same colors as the male, but with a smaller red face mask. Different colors possible. Lightly trilling, warbling song. Climbs nimbly in reeds. Open nester.

Housing: Indoor aviary (32×16×16 in.), in summer also outdoor aviary with a shelter (3×3 ft., no cooler than 65°F / 18°C). Thick reeds and bushes. Provide floor of sand, or concrete with good drainage. Keep food, water, and bathing containers elevated.

Living Conditions: Intolerant of dampness and cold. Twelve- to fourteen-hour day with the aid of a light. Provide ample sunbathing and splashing opportunities. Check claws regularly. Freestanding nest in brush; nesting aids: nesting box, nesting pouches; nest materials: grasses, coconut fibers, and plant wool. Three to six eggs, incubation 12–14 days.

Social Behaviors: Can be kept in several pairs and with other Australian Estrildidae Finches.

Diet: Mixture of various types of millet, plus foxtail millet, canary grass seeds, and grass seeds; grit. During breeding, ample sprout food, half-ripe seeds, and green food.

QUICK INFO Order: *Sparrows* **Family:** *Estrildidae (Waxbills and allies)* (→ p. 18) **Distribution:** *Northern Australia.*

Sudan Golden Sparrow

Auripasser luteus

Housing: 🖼 🗄 🗂
Degree of Difficulty: 1
Voice: ♩
Size: 5¼ in.

Description: Female lighter in color than the male, without the yellow section in feathers. Chirping song. Can quickly become friendly. Lively. Half-cavity nester.

Housing: Cage / indoor aviary (48×20×20 in.) or outdoor aviary with shelter (3×3 ft., no cooler than 50°F / 10°C). Scant vegetation. Provide sand floor. Perches of varying thickness and bowl with fine sand for bathing. Place food, water, and bathing containers on ground.

Living Conditions: Likes to take sand baths. Large, messy nest in thick bush; nesting aids: half-open nesting box; nest materials: plant fibers. May help themselves to nests of other species if they don't have access to sufficient nesting materials. Sensitive to nest checks. Three to four eggs, incubation 11 days. Successful breeders.

Social Behaviors: May be kept with other birds or other seed eaters in an aviary. In cage, keep pair by themselves.

Diet: Seeds rich in carbohydrates (→ p. 246), grass seeds, milk-ripe grains, foxtail millet, green food.

QUICK INFO **Order:** *Sparrows* **Family:** *Weavers* (→ p. 20) **Distribution:** *Mali to Ethiopia.*

Sulfur-crested Cockatoo

Cacatua galerita

Housing: 🏠 🏡
Degree of Difficulty: 2
Voice: 🔊
Size: 16–20 in.

Description: Male and female look the same. The male's iris is brownish black; the female's is reddish brown. Good learners. Cavity nester.

Housing: All-metal indoor or outdoor aviary (9×3×6 ft.), with shelter (6×3 ft., no cooler than 60°F / 15°C). Concrete floor with 6 in. of sand-dirt mixture. Branches for perching and climbing. Provide opportunities to keep busy (→ p. 242); leave flying room. Place food, water, and bathing containers on wall.

Living Conditions: Spray. Change floor covering as needed. Check for worms. Nesting cavity in natural tree trunk or nesting box (16–20×16–20 inches×3–4½ ft., entry hole 5–7 in.). Two to three eggs, incubation 25–27 days.

Social Behaviors: Except during the breeding season, young birds may be kept with other parrots of the same size.

Diet: Seed mixture for cockatoos, manufactured diets (→ p. 246), sprouted food, fruit, vegetables, green food; softwood twigs for gnawing.

QUICK INFO **Order:** *Parrots* **Family:** *Cockatoos (→ p. 7)* **Distribution:** *Large portion of northern, eastern, and southern Australia, Tasmania, New Guinea, surrounding islands.*

Sun Conure

Aratinga solstitialis

Description: Male and female look the same. Fairly loud voice; good mimic. Can become friendly. Cavity nester.

Housing: All metal outdoor aviary (6×3×3 ft., wire thickness ⁵⁄₆₄ in.) with shelter (3×3 ft., no cooler than 50°F / 10°C). Floor concrete. Hardwood branches for perching and climbing; opportunities to keep occupied (→ p. 242). Place food, water, and bathing containers near ground level.

Living Conditions: Robust bird species. Likes to bathe. Mating pair should be able to select each other in flock. Nesting cavity in natural tree trunk (inside diameter 10 in., 16–24 in. deep, entry hole 2½ in.) with extra-thick cavity floor (they gnaw!). Four to six eggs, incubation 24–27 days. Reliable nesters.

Social Behaviors: Aggressive toward other Sun Conures and closely related species, even in adjacent aviary. Some subspecies can be kept with parakeets of comparable size.

Diet: Seed mixture for large parakeets, manufactured diets (→ p. 246), foxtail millet, ripe and half-ripe corncobs, sprouted food, green food, fruits and berries; twigs for gnawing.

Housing:
Degree of Difficulty: 2
Voice:
Size: 12 in.

QUICK INFO Order: *Parrots* Family: *Parrots* (→ p. 6) Distribution: *Southeastern Venezuela, Guyana, northeastern and eastern Brazil.*

Superb Parrot

Polytelis swainsonii

Also: Barraband Parakeet

Housing: 🏛 🗄
Degree of Difficulty: 2
Voice: 🎵 📢))
Size: 16 in.

Description: Female same color as the male, but without yellow on head. Twittering, chortling, warbling voice, loud courtship call; good mimic. Good flier; often spends time on ground. Cavity nester.

Housing: Indoor or outdoor aviary (9×3×6 ft., wire thickness ⁵⁄₆₄ in.) with shelter (6×3 ft., no cooler than 50°F / 10°C). Sprinkler. Floor sand. Branches for perching and climbing. Food, water, and bathing containers on ground.

Living Conditions: Likes to bathe. Tendency toward eye infections. Check regularly for worms. Nesting cavity in natural tree trunk or nesting box (10–12×10–12×24 in., entry hole 3 in.), put in decayed wood. Four to six eggs, incubation 20 days.

Social Behaviors: May be kept with other parakeets and birds of other families.

Diet: Seed mixture for large parakeets, manufactured diets (→ p. 246), foxtail millet, half-ripe weed and grass seeds, sprouted food, green food, fruits; twigs for gnawing.

QUICK INFO Order: *Parrots* Family: *Parrots* (→ p. 6)
Distribution: *Southeastern Australia: Victoria and southern New South Wales.*

Superb Starling

Lamprotornis superbus

Also: *Lamprospreo superbus*

Housing: 🏠 🏡
Degree of Difficulty: 2
Voice: 🎵
Size: 7–8¼ in.

Description: Male and female look the same. Whistling, chattering, twittering song; good imitators. Lively and curious. Cavity nester.

Housing: Indoor aviary (48×24×36 in.) or outdoor aviary with shelter (3×3 ft., no cooler than 68°F / 20°C). Thick vegetation. Floor lined with birdcage litter. Place food, water, and bathing containers on the ground.

Living Conditions: Robust. Gains weight without adequate exercise. Likes to bathe. Mating pair should be able to select each other in flock. Large nest in nesting box (10×10×14 in.; entry hole 2–2½ in. below top edge); nest materials: plant fibers, leaves, roots, hay, and feathers. Three to four eggs, incubation 13–14 days.

Social Behaviors: May be kept in aviary with other Superb Starlings and fairly large bird species, but not with smaller birds.

Diet: Fruits and berries, green food, coarse soft foods containing insects, hamburger, live food.

QUICK INFO Order: *Sparrows* Family: *Starlings* (→ p. 21)
Distribution: *Sudan, Ethiopia, Somalia, Uganda, Kenya, and Tanzania.*

Thick-billed Euphonia

Euphonia laniirostris

Housing:
Degree of Difficulty: 2
Voice: 🎵
Size: 4–5 in.

Description: Male blue-black on topside, female olive green. Song: pleasant twittering, variable warbling; male and female mock. Lively. Open nester.

Housing: Indoor aviary (32×16×16 in.) or outdoor aviary with shelter (3×3 ft., no cooler than 59°F / 15°C). Thick vegetation, including shoots, and flower bulbs. Floor dirt or concrete; good drainage. Keep food, water, and bathing containers elevated.

Living Conditions: Sensitive to damp cold. Domed nest in vegetation or in recesses; nesting aids: half-open nesting box, nesting basket; nest materials: dried grasses, thin twigs, moss, leaves, and coconut fibers. Three to five eggs, incubation 14–15 days. Breeding attempts frequently successful. Mating pair should be able to select each other in flock.

Social Behaviors: Occasionally incompatible with others of its own or related species, so keep mating pair by themselves.

Diet: Fruit, berries, vegetables, green food, nectar drink, soft and live foods, sometimes only spiders.

QUICK INFO **Order:** *Sparrows* **Family:** *Buntings* (→ p. 15) **Distribution:** *Costa Rica and Venezuela, Peru, and Bolivia to Brazil.*

Tiger Finch

Amandava amandava

Housing: 🏠 🏢
Degree of Difficulty: 1
Voice: 🎵
Size: 3½–4 in.

Description: In display plumage, male is red, brown, and black; in standard plumage, lighter like female. Twittering, warbling song; good mimic; even females sing. Good climber. Open nester.

Housing: Indoor or outdoor aviary (32×16×16 in.) with shelter (3×3 ft., no cooler than 68°F / 20°C). Vegetation consisting of bushes, reeds, tall grass. Leave open area on ground. Floor sand with good drainage. Place food, water, and bathing containers near ground level.

Living Conditions: Twelve- to fourteen-hour day with aid of light. Check claws regularly. Freestanding nest in vegetation; nesting aids: nesting basket; nest materials: grasses, raffia, coconut fibers, plant wool, feathers. Four to seven eggs, incubation 11–13 days.

Social Behaviors: During mating season male is often cantankerous, so keep breeding pair separate. Peaceable otherwise.

Diet: Small-grained varieties of millet; canary grass seed; foxtail millet; ripe, half-ripe, and sprouted weed and grass seeds; green food; live food; grit in limited amounts.

QUICK INFO **Order:** *Sparrows* **Family:** *Estrildidae (Waxbills and allies)* (→ p. 18) **Distribution:** *Myanmar, Thailand, Indochina, southwestern China to Bali, Java, Lesser Sunda Islands.*

Trumpeter Finch

Rhodopechys githaginea

Housing:
Degree of Difficulty: 1
Voice: ♩
Size: 4³⁄₄–5¹⁄₄ in.

Also: ***Bucanetes githagineus***

Description: Male in display plumage sand colored with a tinge of pink; in plain plumage like female without pink. Song like tooting of a toy trumpet. Open nester.

Housing: Indoor or outdoor aviary (32×16×16 in.) with shelter (3×3 ft., no cooler than 59°F / 15°C). Floor sand and gravel, large stones, dried grass and a few shrubs. Place food, water, and bathing containers on ground.

Living Conditions: Twelve- to fourteen-hour day with aid of UV light. Freestanding nest on ground or low in vegetation; nesting aids: nesting basket; nest materials: dried plant fibers and leaves, grasses. Four to six eggs, incubation 13–14 days.

Social Behaviors: Peaceable. May be kept with other Trumpeter Finches and other small birds.

Diet: Small seeds containing carbohydrates and mainly oils (→ p. 246), weed and grass seeds, foxtail millet, sprouted food, green food, fruits and berries, fresh twigs with buds, live food; grit in small amounts.

QUICK INFO **Order:** *Sparrows* **Family:** *Finches (→p. 17)*
Distribution: *Canary Islands, southeastern Spain, Africa across the Sahara and Egypt to northwestern India, Caspian Sea to the Altai.*

Turquoise Parrot

Neophema pulchella

Housing: [icons]
Degree of Difficulty: 1
Voice: [icon]
Size: 8–9 in.

Description: Female the same color as the male, but without red wing spot. Soft, quiet whistling voice. Good flier. Cavity nester.

Housing: Indoor or outdoor aviary (36×18×18 in.) with shelter (36×18 in., no cooler than 64°F / 18°C). Sparse vegetation, with floor of short grass. Branches for perching and climbing. Keep food, water, and bathing containers elevated.

Living Conditions: Likes to bathe. Nesting cavity in natural tree trunk or nesting box (8×8×14 in., entry hole 1½–2½ in.); put in peat moss or small-animal litter; nest materials: small grass stems. Four to five eggs, incubation approximately 20 days.

Social Behaviors: Aggressive toward other Turquoise Parrots and closely related species, even in adjacent aviary. May be kept with Estrildidae, doves, or chickens.

Diet: Seed mixture for large parakeets, manufactured diets (→ p. 246), foxtail millet, sprouted food, green food, fruits and vegetables; fresh twigs for gnawing.

QUICK INFO Order: *Parrots* **Family:** *Parrots* (→ p. 6) **Distribution:** *Eastern Australia: northern Victoria to southern Queensland.*

Umbrella Cockatoo

Cacatua alba

Housing: 🏠🏠🏠
Degree of Difficulty: 2
Voice: 🔊
Size: 18 in.

Also: White Cockatoo

Description: Male and female look the same; females have smaller heads; reddish irises. Loud, harsh voice; strong flier; hard chewer.

Housing: Cage or indoor aviary (36×36×48 in.); outdoor aviary with shelter (18×6×6 ft., at least 41°F / 5°C). Wooden perches; regular supply of wood for chewing; provide food, water, and bathing containers off the ground.

Living Conditions: Likes showers, bathing. Cavity brooder; hardwood nest box (22×18×15 in.); one to two eggs, incubation 28–30 days.

Social Behaviors: Male frequently aggressive to mate during breeding season. Avoid colony situations; often aggressive to other species.

Diet: Seed mixture for cockatoos, manufactured diets, sprouts, nuts, greens, vegetables, some fruits, vitamin and mineral supplements.

QUICK INFO Order: *Parrots* **Family:** *Parrots* (→ p. 6)
Distribution: *Indonesia.*

Verditer Flycatcher

Muscicapa thalassina

Also: *Eumiyas thalassina*

Description: Male predominantly greenish blue and black, female a duller green-gray color. Melodious song. Can become friendly. Lively. Hunts insects from a lookout. Cavity nester.

Housing: Indoor or outdoor aviary (6×3×6 ft.) with shelter (3×3 ft., no cooler than 59°F / 15°C); vegetation consisting of low bushes; stones and roots on ground; natural wood perches; leave adequate flying room. Keep food, water, and bathing containers elevated.

Living Conditions: Robust, but sensitive to moisture and cold. Nests near ground level or on ground in half-cavity nesting boxes or nesting basket; nest materials: moss, fine roots, plant fibers, animal hair. Four eggs, incubation 12–14 days.

Social Behaviors: Peaceable. May be kept with other small birds.

Diet: Live food, soft food. Also berries, such as wild grapes except during mating season.

Housing: 🏠 🏛
Degree of Difficulty: 2
Voice: 🎵
Size: 6 in.

QUICK INFO **Order:** *Sparrows* **Family:** *Flycatchers* (→ *p. 14*) **Distribution:** *Kashmir and central China in the north to Malaysia, Sumatra, and Borneo.*

Violet-eared Waxbill

Uraeginthus granatinus

Housing: 🏠 🏢
Degree of Difficulty: 3
Voice: 🎵
Size: 5–5½ in.

Description: Female colored like male, but underside lighter. Twittering, slurred, warbling song; female sings also. Open nester.

Housing: Indoor aviary (48×20×20 in.) or outdoor aviary in the sun with shelter (3×3 ft., no cooler than 77°F / 25°C). Vegetation consisting of bushes. Floor sand or concrete; good drainage. Food, water, and bathing containers near ground.

Living Conditions: Loves warmth and sunshine. Twelve- to fourteen-hour day with aid of light. Mating pair should be free to select each other from flock. Freestanding nest in underbrush; nesting aids: commercially made nest, half-open nesting box; nest materials: coconut fibers, soft grasses, grass cuttings, roots. Three to five eggs, incubation 13 days. Difficult to breed, because the young need lots of warmth.

Social Behaviors: Male aggressive toward other Violet-eared Waxbills and closely related species. May be kept with other Estrildidae finches.

Diet: Small- and large-grained varieties of millet, canary grass seed, soaked wheat and oats, foxtail millet, sprouted food, weed and grass seeds, green food; grit in limited amounts.

QUICK INFO **Order:** *Sparrows* **Family:** *Estrildidae (Waxbills and allies)* (→ p. 18) **Distribution:** *Southern Africa.*

Whiskered Yuhina

Yuhina flavicollis

Housing: [icons]
Degree of Difficulty: 1
Voice: [icon]
Size: 5 in.

Description: Male and female look the same. Subspecies Whiskered Yuhina with yellowish neck band; white necked Yuhina has whitish neck band. Warbling, whispering song. Curious. Lively. Open nester.

Housing: Indoor or outdoor aviary (6×3×6 ft.) with shelter (3×3 ft., no cooler than 59°F / 15°C). Thick vegetation; natural wood perches. Floor of birdcage litter or beech wood chips. Keep food, water, and bathing containers elevated.

Living Conditions: Easy keepers. Change or clean floor covering and furnishings every day or two. Nest in undergrowth; nesting aids: nesting block, nesting basket; nest materials: plant fibers, leaves, moss, fine roots. Two to three eggs, incubation 11–12 days. Breeding attempts commonly successful.

Social Behaviors: Incompatible with other Yuhinas and related species. May be kept with birds of other groups.

Diet: Fine soft foods, nectar drink, cracker softened in water and honey, fruits, berries.

QUICK INFO Order: *Sparrows* Family: *Babblers* (→ p. 14) Distribution: *Himalayas east to Myanmar, northern Indochina and southwestern China.*

White-bellied Canary Finch

Serinus dorsostriatus

Also: *Ochrospiza dorsostriata*

Description: Female not as brightly colored as the male. Loud twittering, trilling song. Open nester.

Housing:
Degree of Difficulty: 1
Voice:
Size: 5 in.

Housing: Cage or indoor aviary (32×16×16 in.) or protected outdoor aviary with shelter (3×3 ft., no cooler than 59°F / 15°C). Thick vegetation with bushes; leave open areas. Floor sand with good drainage. Place food, water, and bathing containers near ground level.

Living Conditions: Initially shy, so provide hiding place of twigs. Easy keeper. Freestanding nest in vegetation; nesting aids: nesting basket, commercially manufactured nest, half-open nesting box; nest materials: grasses, plant fibers, animal and plant wool, feathers. Three to four eggs, incubation 14–15 days. Reliable nester.

Social Behaviors: Peaceable. May be kept with other White-bellied Canary Finches and other small birds.

Diet: Weed and grass seeds containing mostly oils and a little carbohydrate (→ p. 246), foxtail millet, sprouted food, green food, fruits and berries, live food, fresh twigs with buds; grit in limited amounts.

QUICK INFO **Order:** *Sparrows* **Family:** *Finches* (→ p. 17)
Distribution: *East Africa from Tanzania to Ethiopia and Somalia.*

White-capped Pionus

Pionus senilis

Also: White-capped Parrot

Description: Male and female look the same. Avoids the ground. Fast, agile fliers. Shrill voice. Cavity brooder. Not hard chewer.

Housing: Cage or indoor aviary (22×28×15 in.); outdoor aviary (9×3×6 ft., at least 50°F / 10°C); bare floor with good drainage. Provide food and water containers off the ground; perches, swings, branches.

Living Conditions: May prefer showers to bathing. Sometimes reluctant to breed. Wooden nest box (12×12×24 in., entry hole 4 in.) with pine shavings. Four to five eggs, incubation 26 days.

Social Behaviors: More temperamental than other Pionus species. Cautious; easily stressed in new situations.

Diet: Seed mixture for large parrots, manufactured diets, fruits and vegetables, nuts, sprouts, nutritional supplements.

Housing:
Degree of Difficulty: 2
Voice:
Size: 9½ in.

QUICK INFO Order: *Parrots* Family: *Parrots* (→ p. 6)
Distribution: *Mexico, Panama.*

White-cheeked Bulbul

Pycnonotus leucogenys

Housing: ⊞ ⊞
Degree of Difficulty: 1
Voice: 🎵))))
Size: 7 in.

Description: Male and female look the same. Melodious, fairly loud song. Open nester.

Housing: Indoor aviary (48×24×36 in.) or outdoor aviary sheltered from draft, with frost-free shelter (3×3 ft.). Thick vegetation with low bushes, deciduous and evergreen undergrowth. Absorbent floor covering because of runny droppings (birdcage litter or beech wood chips). Food, water, and bathing containers elevated.

Living Conditions: Easy keeper. Freestanding nest in vegetation; nesting aids: nesting basket or half-open nesting box; nest materials: plant fibers, fine roots, animal hairs, and grasses. Sensitive to nest checks. Two to five eggs, incubation 12–13 days. Successful breeding attempts.

Social Behaviors: During mating season incompatible with other birds, so keep mating pair by themselves. At other times, may be kept with other fruit and insect eaters.

Diet: Soft foods containing insects, occasional hamburger, nectar drink, fruits and berries, green foods, live and egg food.

QUICK INFO **Order:** *Sparrows* **Family:** *Bulbuls* (→ p. 11)
Distribution: *Arabian Peninsula, Israel and across Iraq to northern India and Assam.*

White-crested Laughing Thrush

Garrulax leucolophus

Housing: 🏠
Degree of Difficulty: 1
Voice: 🎵
Size: 12–12¼ in.

Description: Male and female look the same; erectile white feather crest. Song a loud, cackling chortling, whistling laugh; females also sing. Climbs enthusiastically in vegetation, also spends time on ground. Curious. Open nesters.

Housing: Outdoor aviary (6×3×6 ft.) with frost-free shelter (3×3 ft.). Thick vegetation with bamboo, bushes, and climbing plants. Floor sand with good drainage. Food, water, and bathing containers near ground level.

Living Conditions: Robust, undemanding. Freestanding nest in vegetation; nesting aids: half-open nesting box or planted hanging flowerpot; nest materials: grass, moss, leaves, and root fibers. Two to five eggs, incubation 13–14 days. Nesting attempts rarely successful.

Social Behaviors: Cantankerous. May be kept only with bird species of equal or larger size.

Diet: Coarse soft foods with high insect component, fruits and berries, green food, live food only during mating season; small bowl with grit.

QUICK INFO Order: *Sparrows* Family: *Babblers* (→ p. 14) Distribution: *Himalayas to western China, through Mayanmar, Thailand, and Indochina to Sumatra.*

White-eared Conure

Pyrrhura leucotis

Description: Male and female look alike. Swift fliers. Quiet voice.

Housing: Cage or indoor aviary (18×18×24 in.); outdoor aviary (9×3×6 ft., shelter 3×3×6 ft., at least 40°F / 5°C). Provide food, water, and bathing containers off the ground. Branches for perching, chewing, and climbing; nest box for sleeping.

Living Conditions: Likes to bathe. Willing breeder. Wooden nest box (10×10×10 in.). Four to six eggs, incubation 23 days.

Social Behaviors: Sometimes aggressive; territorial of cage. Pairs bond easily.

Diet: Seed mixture for large parakeets; manufactured diets; fruits and vegetables; sprouts; calcium, mineral, and vitamin supplements.

Housing: 🏠 🏠 🏠
Degree of Difficulty: 2
Voice: 🔊
Size: 8¾ in.

QUICK INFO Order: *Parrots* Family: *Parrots* (→ p. 6)
Distribution: *Brazil, Venezuela.*

213

White-haired Munia

Lonchura maja

Also: *Munia maja*

Description: Female the same color as the male, but green-white head. First part of song nearly inaudible, second part giggle. Lively; likes to fly. Open nester.

Housing: Indoor aviary (32×16×16 in.) or outdoor aviary with shelter (3×3 ft., no cooler than 64°F / 18°C). Thick vegetation with bushes and reeds; floor sand with good drainage. Place food, water, and bathing containers near ground level.

Living Conditions: Easy keeper. Undemanding. Twelve- to fourteen-hour day with aid of light. Likes to bathe. Check claws. Becomes sluggish in cage. Mating pair should be able to select each other in flock. Nest in vegetation; nesting aids: half-open or closed nesting box; nest materials: grass, plant fibers, roots. Four to seven eggs, incubation 13–15 days.

Social Behaviors: May be kept with several mating pairs and with other Estrildidae.

Diet: Various varieties of millet, canary grass seed, Niger seed, foxtail millet, sprouted food, green food, live food; grit in limited amounts.

Housing:
Degree of Difficulty: 1
Voice:
Size: 4³⁄₈ in.

QUICK INFO Order: *Sparrows* **Family:** *Estrildidae (Wax-bills and allies) (→ p. 18)* **Distribution:** *Southern Thailand, Malaysia, Sumatra and islands, Java, Bali.*

White-rumped Shama

Copsychus malabaricus

Housing: 🏠 🏛 🏚
Degree of Difficulty: 1
Voice: 🎵
Size: 10–11 in.

Description: Female smaller than male, colored brownish gray instead of blackish blue; male's tail is approximately 6 in. long. Varied, melodious song; good mimic; female also sings. Can become friendly. Half-cavity nester.

Housing: Box cage or indoor aviary (39×20×30 in.) or outdoor aviary with shelter (3×3 ft., no cooler than 68°F / 20°C). Thick vegetation, or twigs fastened to mesh. Floor dirt with grass, stones, branches, and twigs. In cage, provide bowl with sprouted grass seed. Only a few branches for perching. Place food, water, and bathing containers on ground.

Living Conditions: Undemanding. Likes to bathe. Nesting aids: half-cavity, commercial cage; nesting materials: twigs, stems, raffia, moss, plant fibers, animal hair. Four to six eggs, incubation 11–12 days.

Social Behaviors: During breeding season sometimes cantankerous with other White-rumped Shamas. May be kept with other seed eaters or individually in cage.

Diet: Coarse soft food for thrushes, live food and egg food, green food, fruits and berries; grit in limited amounts.

QUICK INFO **Order:** *Sparrows* **Family:** *Thrushes* (→ p. 13)
Distribution: *Sri Lanka, India to Thailand, across Malaysia to Borneo.*

215

Yellow-billed Grosbeak

Coccothraustes migratoria
Also: Chinese Grosbeak,
Eophonia migratoria

Housing: **Degree of Difficulty:** 2 **Voice:** ♩ **Size:** 7½–8 in.

Description: Female same color as the male, but gray head. Monotone twittering song. Lively. Open nester.

Housing: Indoor aviary (48×20×20 in.) or outdoor aviary with shelter (3×3 ft., no cooler than 50°F / 10°C). Thick vegetation. Forked branches for perching. Floor sand, good drainage. Keep food, water, and bathing containers elevated.

Living Conditions: At first birds are rambunctious, so keep them in a cage with a soft top. Freestanding nest in angle between branches and tree trunk; nesting aids: nesting basket placed high; nesting materials: twigs, grasses, moss, animal and plant wool. Four eggs, incubation 13–14 days. Successful breeding attempts.

Social Behaviors: Peaceable. May be kept with other Yellow-billed Grosbeaks and other small birds.

Diet: Small seeds containing carbohydrates and mainly oils (→ p. 246); seeds from deciduous trees, weeds, and grasses; foxtail millet; sprouted food; green food; fruits and berries; fresh twigs with buds; live food; grit in small amounts.

QUICK INFO **Order:** *Sparrows* **Family:** *Finches* (→ *p. 17*)
Distribution: *Southeastern Siberia, Manchuria to Korea, southern China, eastern Mayanmar, northern Laos, North Vietnam.*

Yellow Canary

Serinus Flaviventris

Also: *Crithagra flaviventris*

Description: Female more brown than the male. Variable trilling, twittering, whispering, and rolling song. Open nester.

Housing: Indoor aviary (32×16×16 in.) or outdoor aviary with shelter (3×3 ft., no cooler than 50°F / 10°C). Thick vegetation with grasses, few bushes. Floor sand or concrete; good drainage. Food, water, and bathing containers on ground.

Living Conditions: Likes to bathe. Mating pair should be able to select each other in flock. Nest in undergrowth; nesting aids: nesting basket; nest materials: grasses, animal and plant wool, hair, coconut and sisal fibers. Three to four eggs, incubation 13 days.

Social Behaviors: Incompatible with yellow species. May be kept with other small birds.

Diet: Seeds containing oils and carbohydrates (→ p. 246), weed and grass seeds, foxtail millet, sprouted and soaked foods, green food, lots of fruit and berries, fresh branches, live food; grit in limited amounts.

Housing:

Degree of Difficulty: 1

Voice:

Size: 5–5½ in.

QUICK INFO **Order:** *Sparrows* **Family:** *Finches* (→ p. 17) **Distribution:** *Angola to northwest Zimbabwe, the south of South Africa, naturalized in the United States.*

Yellow-crowned Amazon

Amazona ochrocephala

Housing: 🏠 🏛
Degree of Difficulty: 2
Voice: 🔊
Size: 14–15 in.

Description: Male and female look the same. Several possible color variations in the Panama-Amazon subspecies (*A.o. panamensis*). Loud voice, good imitators. Cavity nester.

Housing: All-metal indoor or outdoor aviary (6 × 3×3 ft.; wire thickness ⁵⁄₆₄ in.) with shelter (3×3 ft., no cooler than 50°F / 10°C). Floor sand or concrete with good drainage. Branches for perching and climbing; provide something to keep birds occupied (→ p. 242). Keep food, water, and bathing containers elevated.

Living Conditions: Likes to bathe. Nesting cavity in nesting box (14×24–32×14 in., entry hole 4–4¾ in.). Two to three eggs, incubation approximately 26 days. Successful breeding attempts.

Social Behaviors: Keep mating pair by themselves during breeding season. Except during breeding season, may be kept with other Amazons and birds of other species.

Diet: Seed mixture for Amazons, manufactured diets (→ p. 246), sprouted food, half-ripe seeds, green food, fruit, vegetables; branches with buds for gnawing.

QUICK INFO **Order:** *Parrots* **Family:** *Parrots* (→ p. 6) **Distribution:** *Mexico to Panama, Colombia, and Guyana to northern Bolivia.*

Yellow-crowned Parrot

Cyanoramphus auriceps

Housing:
Degree of Difficulty: 1
Voice: ♩
Size: 9 in.

Description: Yellow less conspicuous in female. Soft, bleating voice like a goat. Dig in ground. Cavity nester.

Housing: Indoor or outdoor aviary (36×18×18 in., wire thickness ¾₄ in.) with frost-free shelter (36×18 in.). Vegetation consisting of bushes; open ground area with sod and mixture of sand and dirt, plus climbing branches. Place food, water, and bathing containers near ground level.

Living Conditions: Undemanding and robust. Likes to bathe. Change floor covering frequently. Check regularly for worms. Reliable nester. Nesting cavity in nesting box (10×10×12 in., entry hole 2½ in.); put in some wood shavings or peat moss. Five to nine eggs, incubation 19–20 days.

Social Behaviors: Keep mating pair by themselves during breeding season. At other times, may be kept with small parakeets.

Diet: Seed food for large parakeets, manufactured diets (→ p. 246), foxtail millet, regular sprouted food and green food, fruits, berries, vegetables, occasionally a whole half-ripe corncob, soft food.

QUICK INFO Order: *Parrots* Family: *Parrots (→ p. 6)*
Distribution: *New Zealand and surrounding islands.*

Yellow-eyed Babbler

Chrysomma sinense

Housing: 🏠 🏦
Degree of Difficulty: 2
Voice: 🎵
Size: 6½–6¾ in.

Description: Male and female look alike. Song is a varied warbling and chattering. Can become very friendly. Fond of exercise. Uses its feet for help in devouring larger insects. Open nester.

Housing: Indoor or outdoor aviary (6×3×6 ft.) with shelter (3×3 ft., no cooler than 60°F / 15°C). Thick vegetation for hiding places; natural wood perches. Birdcage litter floor covering. Keep food, water, and bathing containers elevated.

Living Conditions: Easy keeper. Bathes a lot. Replace perches regularly. At night the birds cling to the cage wire or to vertical branches. Breeds only in aviaries with lots of vegetation. Nest in thick vegetation; nesting aid: nesting basket; nest materials: grasses, plant fibers. Three to five eggs, incubation 13–14 days.

Social Behaviors: Incompatible with other Babblers and related species. Keep with other birds.

Diet: Soft foods containing insects, live food, egg food, fruits and berries (don't cut up the fruit too small).

QUICK INFO Order: *Sparrows* **Family:** *Babblers* (→ p. 14) **Distribution:** *Sri Lanka, from Pakistan and India to southern China.*

Yellow-fronted Canary

Serinus mozambicus

Housing:
Degree of Difficulty: 1
Voice: ♫
Size: 4½–4¾ in.

Also: *Ochrospiza mozambica*

Description: Female same color as the male, but less bright. Melodious song. Lively. Open nester.

Housing: Indoor aviary (32×16×16 in.) or outdoor aviary with shelter (3×3 ft., no cooler than 50°F / 10°C). Vegetation, including bushes and small trees. Floor sand; adequate drainage. Food, water, and bathing containers on ground.

Living Conditions: Robust species, easy keepers. Nest in undergrowth; nesting aids: half-open nesting box, commercially manufactured nest; nest materials: grasses, coconut and sisal fibers, flock, animal and plant wool, feathers. Three to four eggs, incubation 13–14 days.

Social Behaviors: Cantankerous during mating season, during which breeding pair should be kept separate. At other times may be kept with other finches.

Diet: Seeds containing oils and carbohydrates (→ p. 246), weed and grass seeds, foxtail millet, sprouted food, green food, fruits and berries, live food; fresh twigs with buds for gnawing; grit in limited amounts.

QUICK INFO **Order:** *Sparrows* **Family:** *Finches* (→ p. 17) **Distribution:** *South of the Sahara, not in Somalia, in the Congo Basin, in large sections of Namibia, Botswana, South Africa.*

Yellow-fronted Kakariki

Cyanoramphus auriceps

Also: Yellow-fronted Parakeet

Description: Male and female look alike; juveniles have duller head coloration. Several possible colors. Feeds occasionally on the ground. Quiet voice. Strong fliers.

Housing: Cage or indoor aviary (18×18×24 in.); outdoor aviary (10×3×6 ft., provide shelter); concrete floor. Provide food and water containers on ground.

Living Conditions: Check often for worms. Enjoys bathing. Cavity nester; breeds readily. Nest box (8×8×14 in.). Four to twelve eggs; incubation 19–20 days.

Social Behaviors: Aggressive during breeding season. Mischievous, playful, independent.

Diet: Seed mixture for small parakeets, manufactured diets, fruits and vegetables, sprouted seeds, vitamin C and mineral supplements.

Housing:

Degree of Difficulty: 2

Voice: ♩

Size: 9 in.

QUICK INFO Order: *Parrots* Family: *Parrots* (→ p. 6)
Distribution: *New Zealand and outlying islands.*

Yellow-naped Amazon

Amazona o. auropalliata

Housing:	
Degree of Difficulty: 2	
Voice:	
Size: 15 in.	

Description: Male and female look similar; juveniles without yellow on nape. Strong fliers. Loud voice. Hard chewer. Cavity brooders.

Housing: Cage or indoor aviary (30×30×36 in.) or outdoor aviary (12×4½×6 ft.) with shelter (4½×3×6 ft., at least 50°F / 10°C). Provide food, water, and bathing containers off the floor; natural branches for climbing and perching.

Living Conditions: Likes to bathe. Needs regular supply of wood for chewing. Nesting box (12×12×20 in.). Two to four eggs; incubation 26 days.

Social Behaviors: Friendly, playful. Becomes extremely aggressive while breeding.

Diet: Seed mixture for Amazons, manufactured diets, fruits and vegetables, sprouts, wild greens, vitamin and mineral supplements.

QUICK INFO **Order:** *Parrots* **Family:** *Parrots* (→ p. 6)
Distribution: *Costa Rica, Mexico.*

Yellow-rumped Munia

Lonchura flaviprymna

Housing:
Degree of Difficulty: 1
Voice: ♫
Size: 4¼ in.

Description: Male and female look the same. Raw, rasping voice, high twittering and whistling. Lively. Interesting courtship behavior. Open nester.

Housing: Indoor aviary (32×16×16 in.) or outdoor aviary with shelter (3×3 ft., no cooler than 65°F / 18°C). Thick vegetation. Floor sand with good drainage. Place food, water, and bathing containers close to ground level.

Living Conditions: Use lamp to simulate twelve- to fourteen-hour day. Not appropriate for living in a cage—birds gain weight. Mating pair should be allowed to select each other in a flock. Nest in undergrowth; nesting aids: half-open nesting box, nesting block; nest materials: grasses, plant fibers. Four to five eggs, incubation approximately 13 days.

Social Behaviors: Peaceable. May be kept with several mating pairs and with other finches. Do not keep with Chestnut-breasted Mannikin, because they interbreed.

Diet: Varieties of millet, canary grass seed, sprouted food, weed and grass seeds, green food; grit in limited amounts.

QUICK INFO Order: *Sparrows* **Family:** *Estrildidae (Waxbills and allies)* (→ p. 18) **Distribution:** *Northwestern and northern Australia.*

Yellow-rumped Serin

Serinus xanthopygia

Also: *Ochrospiza xanthopygia*

Description: Female similar to male, but not as brightly colored. Twittering, warbling song. Persistent singer. Calm disposition. Open nester.

Housing: Cage or indoor aviary (32×16×16 in.) or outdoor aviary with shelter (3×3 ft., no cooler than 50°F / 10°C). Vegetation consisting of grasses and bushes; leave an open area. Floor sand with good drainage. Place food, water, and bathing containers near ground level.

Living Conditions: Durable. Easy to keep. Freestanding nest in undergrowth; nesting aids: nesting basket, commercially manufactured nest, nesting block; nest materials: dried grasses, plant fibers, sisal and coconut fibers, flax, feathers, flock, moss. Three to four eggs, incubation approximately 14 days. Reliable brooders, even in cage.

Social Behaviors: Incompatible with other Yellow-rumped Serins. May be kept with other small birds.

Diet: Seeds containing oils and mainly carbohydrates (→ p. 246), ripe and half-ripe weed and grass seeds, foxtail millet, green food, live foods; grit in limited quantities.

Housing:
Degree of Difficulty: 1
Voice: ♫
Size: 4¼–4¾ in.

QUICK INFO **Order:** *Sparrows* **Family:** *Finches* (→ p. 17)
Distribution: *Northern and western Ethiopia.*

Yellow-winged Pytilia

Pytilia hypogrammica

Description: Female the same color as the male, but with hardly any red on head. Song: squeaking, warbling tones. Open nester.

Housing: Indoor aviary (32×16×16 in.) or outdoor aviary with shelter (3×3 ft., no cooler than 68°F / 20°C). Thick vegetation of bushes, reeds, and bamboo, floor sand with good drainage. Place food, water, and bathing containers near ground level.

Living Conditions: Provide opportunities for sunbathing. Twelve- to fourteen-hour day with aid of light. Freestanding nest in undergrowth; nesting aids: half-open nesting box; nest materials: grasses, coconut and sisal fibers, feathers. Three to five eggs, incubation 12–13 days. Reliable nesters.

Social Behaviors: Sometimes aggressive toward other Yellow-winged Pytilias and closely related species; peaceable with other Estrildidae.

Diet: Small-grained varieties of millet, canary grass seed, Niger seed, foxtail millet, sprouted food, green food, live food; grit in limited amounts.

Housing:	🏠 🏤
Degree of Difficulty:	2
Voice:	🎵
Size:	4½–4¾ in.

QUICK INFO **Order:** *Sparrows* **Family:** *Estrildidae (Waxbills and allies)* (→ p. 18) **Distribution:** *Sierra Leone and Ivory Coast to Central African Republic.*

Zebra Dove

Geopelia striata

Housing:		
Degree of Difficulty: 1		
Voice: ♫		
Size: 8–8¾ in.		

Description: Male and female look the same. Trilling call. Can become friendly. Remain on the ground. Open nester.

Housing: Cage or indoor aviary (48×32×48 in.), in the summer also outdoor aviary with shelter (3×3 ft., no cooler than 59°F / 15°C). Plant heavily, but also leave open space on ground. Floor in cage paper, dirt in aviary; bowl with sand for sand bath. Place food, water, and bathing containers near ground level in such a way that they can't be tipped over.

Living Conditions: Undemanding. Bathing with spray or in sand. Flat nest; nesting aids: nesting basket, box open at top among vegetation; nest materials: coconut fibers, twigs, straw, moss. Two eggs, incubation 13 days. Nesting attempts often successful.

Social Behaviors: During mating time incompatible with other Zebra Doves and other doves. May be kept with other bird species.

Diet: Seed mixture for parakeets (→ p. 246), foxtail millet, weed seeds, soft and live food, green food; grit.

QUICK INFO **Order:** *Doves* **Family:** *Doves (→ p. 6)*
Distribution: *India through Southeast Asia to Australia.*

Zebra Finch

Poephila guttata

Also: *Taeniopygia guttata*

Description: Female less conspicuous than the male, sides of head gray. Many possible colors. Trumpeting, chortling, twittering song. Open nester.

Housing: Cage or indoor aviary (32×16×16 in.) or outdoor aviary with shelter (3×3 ft., no cooler than 59°F / 15°C). Thick vegetation; leave an open area. Floor sand with good drainage. Place food, water, and bathing containers near ground level.

Living Conditions: Very undemanding and hardy. Twelve- to fourteen-hour day with aid of light. Likes to bathe. Nesting aids: half-open nesting box, woven raffia basket; nesting materials: grasses, coconut fibers, small feathers. Four to six eggs, incubation 11–13 days. Reliable nester.

Social Behaviors: May be kept with other Zebra Finches and other Estrildidae in large aviary.

Diet: Small- and large-grained varieties of millet, canary grass seed, foxtail millet, weed and grass seeds, sprouted food, green food, and fruit; grit in small amounts.

Housing:		
Degree of Difficulty: 1*		
Voice:		
Size: 4 in.		

QUICK INFO **Order:** *Sparrows* **Family:** *Estrildidae (Waxbills and allies)* (→ p. 18) **Distribution:** *Australia, Lesser Sunda islands.*

Zebra Waxbill

Amandava subflava

Housing:
Degree of Difficulty: 2
Voice: ♩
Size: 3½–4 in.

Description: Female less brightly colored than male, without the red stripe over the eye. Song consists of one note. Lively. Open nester.

Housing: Cage or indoor aviary (32×16×16 in.) or outdoor aviary covered by two-thirds roof with shelter (3×3 ft., no cooler than 60°F / 15°C at night). Vegetation of grasses, stones and roots. Floor sand with good drainage. Place food, water, and bathing containers close to ground level.

Living Conditions: Easy keeper, robust and hardy. Provide twelve- to fourteen-hour day with aid of lamp. Very reliable breeder. Cylindrical nest in vegetation; nesting aid: closed or half-open nesting box; nest materials: stems, raffia, feathers. Takes over nests of other species of Estrildid finches. Three to six eggs, incubation 12–14 days.

Social Behaviors: Aggressive toward other Zebra Waxbills during breeding time. May be kept with other Estrildid finches.

Diet: Small-grained varieties of millet, canary grass seed, soaked wheat and oats, foxtail millet, sprouted food, green food, small live food; grit in limited amounts.

QUICK INFO **Order:** *Sparrows* **Family:** *Estrildidae (Waxbills and allies)* (→ p. 18) **Distribution:** *African steppes and savannas south of the Sahara.*

Around the Bird Home

Depending on size and behavior, the various bird species place individual demands on their accommodations. Here is everything you need to know about setting up cages and aviaries in which your bird is sure to feel at home.

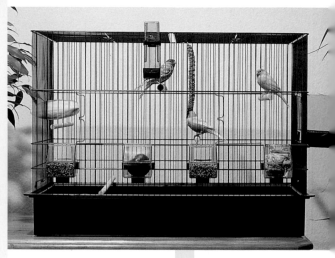

Birdcage

> **Everything a bird needs. Regular exercise is necessary.**

There are many types of cages on the market. Choose one that is suitable for the species of bird you wish to keep. Ideally, the bird should be able to fully extend its wings without touching the bars of the cage, and there should be plenty of headroom with ample clearance for the tail feathers. The cage should be roomy enough to accommodate perches, food and water containers, and toys, all without crowding the bird.

➤ Wire cages open on all sides with a plastic bottom pan or a pullout drawer are appropriate for seed eaters such as canaries. For par-

EXTRA TIP

Cage Location
Well lighted, but not in direct sun. Morning sunshine is good. Bird should get some direct daylight not filtered through glass for a little while every day. Dry, free from draft; airy, but without extreme temperature fluctuations. To keep from frightening the birds, place cage at observers' eye level or higher.

rots, the cage should have horizontal wire bars.

➤ A cage closed on all sides except for the front bars is appropriate for bird species that remain shy, and for use in acclimating new birds. For species that are easily frightened the ceiling can be cushioned with foam rubber, or other soft material.
Floor covering: Wood shavings, birdcage litter, newspaper, absorbent paper towels. Birdcage litters are composed of various things such

CAGE DO'S AND DONT'S

- ✔ Make sure cage is roomy enough; better to be too large than too small.
- ✔ Never crowd birds in a cage meant to house one.
- ✔ Cage wires should match the strength of the bird and spaced appropriately for the occupant.
- ✔ Fresh water must be available at all times in a sturdy container to prevent tips.
- ✔ Remove all stale and contaminated food to prevent illness.

Very healthful: green food for vitamins, a natural wood branch for gymnastics.

as crushed walnut shells, corncob, compacted shredded paper, or wood shavings. Avoid cedar shavings; they emit harsh chemical fumes that are harmful, and can, in some cases, be fatal to birds. When using any of these litters as a substrate in the cage or aviary, make sure there is a grate in the bottom that will restrict your bird's access to the materials. If your bird eats any of these things, it could

Bath-time fun in a pottery bathing bowl. Change water daily.

suffer intestinal impaction, digestion problems, or even death.

Plain black-and-white-newspaper is safe and non-toxic; avoid glossy, colorful papers, as they could contain harmful dyes or chemicals. Other safe papers include brown paper bags cut apart and spread out, paper towels, and (of course) newsprint. You can buy this by the roll at an office or art supply store.

Cage bars

Bars should be anodized; not shiny or coated with plastic. With parrots, match the thickness of the bars to the strength of the beak;

SHOPPING LIST

- ✔ Food and water dishes
- ✔ Bathing bowl
- ✔ Two to three perches, preferably natural wood
- ✔ Nesting aids such as a nesting basket or nesting box
- ✔ Nest materials
- ✔ Floor covering such as beech wood shavings, birdcage litter, or absorbent paper
- ✔ Toys such as ropes, ladders, swings, small bells
- ✔ Potted plants
- ✔ Spray bottle

An eating spot that acts as a swing quickly becomes a favorite place for your birds.

EXTRA TIP

Light in the Birds' Quarters

Birds need adequate daylight or an artificial light that provides the same thing. The best choice is a full-spectrum bulb, which produces a light that comes as close as possible to real sunlight. Like natural sunlight, it contains UV rays, which are important for the synthesis of vitamin D_3. The intensity and duration of daylight (eight to twelve hours) should match the bird's natural home. Electronic devices can be used to reduce the flickering of fluorescent lighting, which is visible to birds.

choose bars that are close enough together so that the bird's head can't fit through; parrots require horizontal bars for climbing.

Furnishings: Food and water containers that can be attached to cage wall (a separate container for each type of food); bathhouse to place in the door or bowl for bathwater; natural wood perches thick enough so that the bird cannot reach all the way around them; objects to keep the birds occupied ($\rightarrow$ p. 242); nesting supplies hung on outside of cage wire.

Lighting: Daylight lamp ($\rightarrow$ Tip, p. 235).

Indoor Aviary

This is usually a larger cage that stands on a base with

> **An indoor aviary offers birds plenty of room for climbing and flying.**

casters. That way the indoor aviary can be pushed onto a balcony or porch. There are several models available in pet shops.

Size: This depends on the species of bird kept. The aviary should be longer than it is wide. For seed eaters and parrots published material is available that deals with nutrition and minimum aviary size (→ Addresses, p. 255).

Floor: Layer of bird sand, gravel, beech wood chips, birdcage litter, or absorbent paper. It must be cleaned or changed regularly—for birds that leave runny droppings, two or three times a week. A base about 4 in. high keeps the floor covering, feathers, and seeds from falling out.

Wire: Wire should be anodized or made of aluminum, and not shiny.

> A wood aviary is appropriate for birds that don't gnaw.

EXTRA TIP

Shelter
A shelter is a walled room isolated from heat and noise attached directly to the outdoor aviary. It should be equipped with a light, a water connection and drain (for more effective cleaning), heat, a humidifier, and emergency lighting. The birds' accommodations for sleeping and nesting are also inside the shelter. With several aviaries it's best to use a food preparation kitchen.

Green wire enhances visibility. For parrots, match wire thickness to beak strength; choose a mesh or bar spacing size small enough so that the birds can't get their heads through.

Setup: Perches should be of natural wood; don't set them up over food or drinking water; be sure to provide plenty of flying room. Depending on bird species, place food, water, and bathing containers in an elevated position or on aviary bars. Attach nesting materials to walls.

The nest is cushioned with fine nest material such as cotton for filters.

SHOPPING LIST

- ✔ Attachments for mesh walls
- ✔ Concrete for walls
- ✔ Concrete or concrete sidewalk slabs for floor
- ✔ Plants, climbing plants
- ✔ Containers for water, food, and bathing
- ✔ Large bowls for sand
- ✔ Branches for perching and climbing
- ✔ Floor covering
- ✔ Nesting aids, nest materials
- ✔ Sprinkler installation, spray bottle

Location: (→ Tip, p. 232).

Outdoor Aviary

This is an aviary set up in the open air. The long side should be oriented toward the south or southeast. About a third of it should be covered with material that allows the passage of light and UV rays.

Size: Size should match the requirements and the size of the bird species kept. A rec-

Nesting baskets are the right nesting aids for open nesters such as canaries.

tangular floor should be no higher than 6 to 8 ft. so you can take good care of the aviary. Usually a shelter is attached (→ Tip p. 236) that the birds enter through a small opening.

Foundation: For protection against rats and mice it's important to use beveled concrete. Another option is to sink a wall 32 in. high about a foot into the ground and place wire mesh over it.

Wire Mesh: Depending on the species, a wood or metal frame is covered with wire.

> **The suspended structure is a favorite flight destination when the birds are loose.**

The thickness of the wire is matched to the strength of the beak and the gnawing habits of the inhabitants (→ bird portraits). Double coverage is sensible protection against cats, martens, owls, and raptors.

Floor Covering: (→ Indoor Aviary, p. 235.)

Furnishings: Bushes, trees, grass, bamboo—on the floor or in buckets. Food, water, and bathing contain-

A play area on the roof of the cage is an invitation to play and eat.

ers on the floor or elevated, made from materials that are easy to clean. Perches made of natural wood, not placed over the food and water containers. Branches or trees for climbing (but don't restrict flying room); sprinkler installation.

Location: With areas of sun and shade; protected from wind and rain.

Flying Indoors

Cage-kept birds should have a couple of hours of exercise outside the cage every day. If your bird has unclipped wings, a daily period of carefully supervised flight is great exercise. That helps them keep their flying muscles in shape and avoids gaining weight. Before the first free flight, you must make the birds' room suitable for flight. Here are a few examples of things to look out for:

➤ Close windows all the way, and at first keep the curtains closed.

➤ Close closet doors and drawers to avoid accidentally shutting the birds inside.

➤ Close doors to the rooms

EXTRA TIP

Before the First Free Flight

Let your birds fly around only after they have settled in and are no longer frightened by your presence. They should also have enough time to inspect their surroundings from inside the cage. Remove all possible dangers in the flight room. If the birds don't venture out of the cage right away when the door is opened, don't shoo them out. Always feed them inside the cage. That way they will always go back inside.

1 **Nesting basket**

2 **Wooden swings**

3 **Rope swing—food enhances the appeal**

4 **Delicious fruit basket**

Sisal swing 5

that look like an invitation to land. The birds' toes could get pinched.

➤ Watch where you walk to avoid stepping on a bird that may have landed on the floor.

➤ Remove narrow, water-filled containers. Birds could drown in them.

➤ Birds could be injured on pointed objects; cover or put away.

➤ Secure electric appliance cords and plugs.

➤ Birds can get burned on pans with hot contents, burning candles, and hot stove burners.

➤ Remove poisonous houseplants.

➤ Supervise any other pets that have access to your bird.

A Play Area for Fliers

To keep your birds from landing everywhere when they are free, you can provide a specific landing place.

➤ Good possibilities for this are the "playgrounds" available in pet shops; these are set on top of the cage or attached to the cage bars.

➤ A great choice is a bird tree, which you can also get at a pet shop. Ideally this

should stand in a corner far away from the cage, to give the birds cover and force them to fly to the tree. You can make these places even more attractive for your feathered friends with ladders, swings, bells, and other items.

Clipped Wings

Birds with clipped wings benefit from regular supervised playtime outside the cage. Play stands or bird trees offer them the oppor-

EXTRA TIP

Safe Flights
Many birds, especially caged ones, enjoy and need flight time to avoid boredom as well as keep in shape. However, they can injure themselves and sometimes even kill themselves if they fly into mirrors and windows. To protect your birds it's a good idea to place decals on or hang a sheer curtain over these shiny attractions. In time, your birds will recognize that these objects are not openings.

tunity to exercise and have fun at the same time. Outfit the play areas with ladders, swings, bells, rope toys, and plenty of things to climb and chew on.

If you have a parrot or a smaller hookbilled bird, such as a budgie or cockatiel, it is a good idea to clip its wings as a safety precaution. This isn't cruel, harmful, or painful, and could save your bird's life by preventing it from flying out open doors or windows, or into dangerous areas such as fireplaces or ceiling fans. Additionally, a bird that is difficult to handle often behaves better with neatly clipped wing feathers.

If you don't know how to clip your bird's wings, have your avian veterinarian teach you. Learn to clip the flight feathers in a manner that allows the bird to glide to the floor; this will prevent if from crashing down and

possibly injuring itself. If you aren't comfortable clipping the feathers yourself or if the bird is too large for you to handle, the veterinarian will clip the wings for you. Bird groomers and some pet stores will also clip your bird's wings. Expect to pay a small fee.

Be aware that some birds (cockatiels and conures, for example) can still fly reasonably well even with clipped wings. Take extra precautions when such a bird is playing outside its cage. Additionally, supervise or lock away other pets while your bird is out.

Keeping Birds Occupied

In their natural environment birds are busy for a major part of the day searching for food and eating. In contrast, birds kept in a cage or an aviary are in the land of milk and honey. Food is delivered to their house at the same time every day, and usually it is

Inseparable mates need small seeds as a staple food.

Grit: Teeth in the Tummy

Hard seeds need to be digested. However, seed eaters don't have teeth to break them into smaller parts. Instead, they have developed a stomach that's capable of "chewing;" it is lined with tissue that acts like a grater. The seed mash is abraded by rhythmic contractions of the stomach muscles. To further aid the process, some seed eaters also need to take in small pebbles or grit. Some birds such as doves and chickens need grit because they swallow their foods whole. You can offer finches, canaries, or similar birds small amounts of grit as long as you are careful not to overfeed. Some birds may eat too much and can suffer impactions or other serious problems. Psittacines, or parrot-type birds, don't require grit because they hull seeds before they eat them.

already reduced to bite-sized pieces for their beaks. As result of this "sweet life" the birds easily put on weight and become sluggish. You need to prevent this.

Using Food to Keep Birds Occupied: Let the bird "prepare" its own food.

The Oriental White-eyes like soft fruit and insects.

➤ Attach branches with rough bark inside the bird home. Chewing the bark is fun for many birds. Note: Carefully clean any fresh branches before giving them to your bird, because they may harbor insects, larvae, parasites, or droppings from diseased wild birds. Collect branches from pesticide-free areas and avoid trees that stand alongside roads, as they are likely contaminated with exhaust fumes or chemicals.

To clean the branches, use a stiff brush and scrub them with a mixture of hot soapy water and a little household bleach. Rinse until no odor of bleach remains, then let dry thoroughly outside in the sun.

➤ Hang a bunch of grass, half-ripe grain, or a bundle of mature weeds gathered from pesticide-free areas on the cage bars. Some gymnastics are required for harvesting the seeds.

"Dainty" table manners: Common Hill Mynahs sling their food around when they eat.

➤Corn on the cob is a fun feeding activity.

➤Skewer pieces of fruits such as bananas, oranges, and apples or attach fruit shish kebabs to the perches or the cage bars.

Toys for Birds

Pet shops offer a wide variety of toys suitable for birds of all species. Here are just a few examples:

➤Thick sisal or hemp ropes can't be pulled to pieces, but the bird can use them for climbing and swinging. Wooden swings are also fun.

➤Wooden or plastic tops can be pushed with the beak.

➤Mesh balls with a little bell not only roll nicely, but also make noise and can be easily carried in the beak. Always choose size-appropriate toys.

Inappropriate Toys

Don't bother with mirrors and plastic birds. Male birds take both their own mirror image and "plastic playmates" to be competitors or partners. Both cause stress, for the rival doesn't fly away, and the courted female doesn't respond properly. Stress can also make birds ill.

Organically Grown Fruits and Berries

Fruits are essential to fruit eaters, and they are important sources of vitamins for many other bird species. But birds are very sensitive to chemicals, so try to get organically grown fruits, which won't contain any poisonous residues. Before feeding conventionally grown fruits, wash them thoroughly. Better yet, peel them, for often the indigestible substances remain on the peels.

Seed Eaters

The seed eaters class includes all birds that eat primarily seeds, such as Estrildidae and fin., weavers, babblers, doves, chickens, and many parrots. Their beaks are adapted to seed foods (→ Tip, p. 17). Seeds contain high biological value. They are easily digested and contain a high nutrient content, which makes them especially high in energy. By husking the seeds before eating them the birds reduce the roughage content. According to their main nutrients, seeds can be divided into two categories:

➤ seeds rich in carbohydrates: millet, rice, canary grass seed, grains, and grass seeds

➤ seeds containing oils: sunflower, poppy, perilla, Niger

This European Robin is looking for an extra helping of insects on the floor of the aviary.

EXTRA TIP

Casts
All insect eaters take in undigestible materials, such as the chitin shells of insects, along with their live food. And like owls, insect eaters also rid themselves of these materials by regurgitating them in the form of a small pellet or cast. Roughage is necessary for the formation of pellets. That's why you need to offer the birds more than such items as egg or cottage cheese.

seed, sesame and linseed, hemp seed, and turnip

Seed eaters don't all eat the same seed mixture, though. Different species have different nutritional requirements. You have to take this into account in feeding the birds. Here are a couple of seed mixtures:

For large parrots: Sunflower, oats, wheat, corn, raw rice, peanuts, and pumpkin seeds. Additionally, tree seeds, nuts, millet, and canary grass seed.

For large parakeets: Sunflower, assorted varieties of millet, canary grass seed; a

little husked oats, hemp seed, and peanuts.

For Amazons: Sunflower, assorted varieties of millet, raw rice, oats, corn, peanuts, and pumpkin seeds.

For Cockatoos: Assorted varieties of millet, canary grass seed, wheat, hemp seed, buckwheat; some sunflower, hemp seed, pumpkin

> **Blackbirds eat primarily insects and small animals.**

seeds, a few nuts.

For Parakeets: Assorted varieties of millet, canary grass seed, foxtail millet; a little hemp seed, Niger seed, and linseed.

EXTRA TIP

Procuring Live Food

Live food is an important source of protein. Birds need this material especially for building their bodies. Young birds in the growth phase and molting birds in particular have a heightened need for protein (the keratin in the feathers is a protein). To provide your birds with live food, you can look for the food yourself or buy it in a pet shop.

Varied Diet

However, seeds are not the only things that many of these birds need to stay healthy. A diet of nothing but seeds can be nutritionally incomplete and lead to serious health issues such as vitamins A and D_3 deficiencies, respiratory infections, skin irritations, and other problems. Manufactured diets such as pelleted or extruded foods are highly recommended, especially for the hook bills.

Pelleted and Extruded Foods

Pelleted and extruded foods contain balanced amounts of nutrients in each piece. The foods are available in a variety of flavors, color, shapes, and scents, and species-specific diets are available. Healthy birds that eat these foods along with regular servings of fresh fruits and vegetables rarely need dietary supplements. Discuss your bird's nutritional requirements with your avian veterinarian. The veterinarian will be happy to help you develop a nutritious meal plan for your bird.

Green and Live Foods

Seed food is only a basic food. To take in adequate nourishment, birds also need green and live food. Green foods include all weeds such as bird pimpernel and dandelion; vegetables such as lettuce, mangel, and cucumbers; and herbs such as parsley. Birds get lots of important minerals, trace elements, and vitamins when they eat green foods. As a replacement for green foods, such as during the nutritionally poor wintertime, you can give the birds sprouted food—seeds that have been sprouted and harvested after the emergence of the seedling. Always harvest any green foods from pesticide-free areas.

Fruit Eaters

Fruit eaters is the term applied to bird species that eat primarily fruits and berries throughout the year. These include such birds as bulbuls, white eyes, lories, starlings, and tanagers. The fruit eaters are likewise anatomically adapted to their food. In contrast to the seed eaters, they are equipped with only a weak muscle or chewing stomach, and only a short small intestine with a broad lumen. As a result, their droppings contain lots of water and are consequently very runny ($\rightarrow$ Tip, p. 12). The sticky food can also build up on the beak and foster fungal infections. Hygiene is therefore very important with fruit eaters. Because fruits generally grow high in trees, the food also needs to be provided to the birds in an elevated position.

You can offer practically any fruits that are available at the market. You should avoid avocados, though, because they are harmful to birds.

Some of the food you can offer cut into small pieces in a bowl; however, you should also offer some of it in halves or whole for "occupational therapy" ($\rightarrow$ p. 244). Not every bird likes its food presented in the same way. Try different possibilities.

Lory Food Specialists

Lories eat primarily nectar and pollen. For that purpose they have a long, narrow tongue with a tip heavily endowed with taste buds. When a lory inserts its tongue into a flower, the taste buds stand up and suck up the nectar like a sponge. When the tongue is brought back into the beak, the sweet juice is expressed into skin folds in the roof of the mouth. As a substitute for nectar, lories get a special food, Lorikeet mix. This is available in pet shops and needs only to be stirred in with a liquid. You can also offer fruit and pollen or live food as a source of protein

Insect Eaters

The insect eaters category includes bird species that eat mainly insects and other invertebrates. Examples are thrushes and flycatchers. Characteristics of insect eaters are a very short, broad beak (swift) and a slender, pointed, occasionally long beak like that of the flycatchers. In many species, bristles around the base of the beak increase the effectiveness of the capturing mechanism. Offer insect eaters primarily live food, that is, larvae of mealworms, lesser mealworms, greater wax moths, fly larvae or maggots, enchytraeid worms, or (larger species) crickets. You should avoid wild food insects to protect possibly endangered species. This is a safety precaution as well; you never know what pesticides they carry.

Food Supplement

Because insect eaters often eat berries in the wild, you can offer your birds berries from mountain ash, elder, and firethorn. In addition, you should gradually get the birds used to soft food. Half is made up of dried insect meal and larvae, mayfly larvae, and egg yolk. The other half consists of grain pellets, wafers or zwieback, green food, and berries mixed together. Before feeding, the food is moistened with low-fat cottage cheese to create a crumbly texture. If you substitute grated apple or carrot for the cottage cheese, you can also give the food to fruit eaters.

EXTRA TIP

Freshness Counts
Warning: Soft foods quickly spoil when moistened. Thus they should always be prepared and served fresh. Throw out uneaten portions within an hour or so.

Imperial/metric conversion chart

⅛ inch = 3 mm	8 inches = 20 cm
¼ inch = 5 mm	8½ inches = 21 cm
½ inch = 1 cm	9 inches = 23 cm
¾ inch = 2 cm	10 inches = 25 cm
1 inch = 2.5 cm	10½ inches = 27 cm
1½ inches = 4 cm	12 inches (1 foot) = 30 cm
2 inches = 5 cm	14 inches = 35 cm
2½ inches = 6 cm	16 inches = 40 cm
3 inches = 7.5 cm	18 inches (1½ feet) = 45 cm
4 inches = 10 cm	20 inches = 50 cm
4½ inches = 12 cm	21 inches = 52 cm
5 inches = 13 cm	24 inches (2 feet) = 60 cm
5½ inches = 14 cm	26 inches = 65 cm
6 inches = 15 cm	27 inches = 68 cm
6¼ inches = 16 cm	30 inches (2½ feet) = 75 cm
6½ inches = 17 cm	36 inches (3 feet) = 90 cm
7 inches = 18 cm	72 inches (6 feet) = 180 cm

Species Index by Latin Names

Subject Index

Resources

Organizations
American Federation of Aviculture, Inc.
P.O. Box 7312
North Kansas City, MO 64116
http://www.afabirds.org/

Association of Avian Veterinarians
P.O. Box 811720
Boca Raton, FL 33481
http://www.aav.org/

Periodicals
Bird Talk Magazine
P.O. Box 6050
Mission Viejo, CA 92690

Birds U.S.A.
P.O. Box 6050
Mission Viejo, CA 92690

Bird Times
Pet Publishing Inc.
7-L Dundas Circle
Greensboro, NC 27407

Books
Athan, Mattie Sue, and Dianalee Deter. *The African Grey Handbook.* Hauppauge, NY: Barron's Educational Series, Inc., 2000.

Vriends, Matthew. *The Canary Handbook.* Hauppauge, NY: Barron's Educational Series, Inc., 2001.

Vriends, Matthew, Ph.D. *The Cockatiel Handbook.* Hauppauge, NY: Barron's Educational Series, Inc., 1999.

Watkins, Anne C. *The Conure Handbook.* Hauppauge, NY: Barron's Educational Series, Inc., 2004.

Koepff, Christa, and April Romagnano. *The Finch Handbook.* Hauppauge, NY: Barron's Educational Series, Inc., 2001.

Gorman, Mary. *Lovebirds.* Hauppauge, NY: Barron's Educational Series, Inc., 2005.

Lantermann, Werner. *Cockatoos.* Hauppauge, NY: Barron's Educational Series, Inc., 2000.

Lantermann, Werner. *Amazon Parrots.* Hauppauge, NY: Barron's Educational Series, Inc., 2000.

Birmelin, Immanuel. *Budgerigars.* Hauppauge, NY: Barron's Educational Series, Inc., 1998.

Web Sites

http://www.birdsnways.com/
http://www.upatsix.com/
http://www.finchworld.com
http://www.nfss.org/
http://www.cockatiels.org
http://www.budgies.org/
http://www.parrotparrot.com
http://www.conure.org
http://www.amazonasociety.org/
http://www.africangreys.com
http://www.arndt-verlag.com
http://www.fws.gov

Appendix

Cover Photo: Gouldian Finch; **Back Cover:** Fischer's Lovebird (top), Red-headed Finch (middle), Blue and Gold Macaw (bottom)

Inside Photo Credits

Anders; Angermayer: Reinhard, Schmidt, Wendl, Ziesler; Arco Images: Layer, Sohns, Schulte; Ardea: Avon, England, Gohier, Parer/Parer-Cook, Steyn, Trouson, Watson, Zipp; Behling; Bielfeld; Bucsis/Somerville; Cramm; Francais; Giel, Hecker: Mestel; Juniors: Bauer, Bielfeld, Born, Brehm, Giel, Haas, Klapp, Koch, Layer, Maier, Schmidbauer, Schulte, Steimer, Thielscher, Thumann, Wegner; Lancione; Okapia: Bentsen, Bowers/Wildlife, Prenzel; Pfeffer; Pieter; Reinhard; Robiller; Schmidbauer; Silvestris online: A.N.T., Brandl, Brehm, Hecker, Hosking, Layer, Malowski, Sohns, Walz, Wilmhurst; Skogstad; Univision; Webb; Wegler; Wothe; Zeininger